The Politics of Redemption:

The Doctrine, the Matter, the Law, and Grace

THE PÈRE MARQUETTE
LECTURE IN THEOLOGY
2025

THE POLITICS OF REDEMPTION:

THE DOCTRINE, THE MATTER,
THE LAW, AND GRACE

by

M. SHAWN COPELAND

Professor Emerita of Systematic Theology
Boston College

Library of Congress Control Number: 2025931180

Names: M. Shawn Copeland, Author
Title: The Politics of Redemption: The Doctrine, the Matter, the Law, and Grace
Series: Père Marquette Lecture in Theology: 55

Identifiers: LCCN 2025931180 | ISBN 9781626005204

© 2025 Marquette University Press
Milwaukee WI 53201-3141
All rights reserved.
Manufactured in the United States of America
Founded 1916
www.marquette.edu/mupress/

EU Authorised Representative: Mare Nostrum Group B.V.,
Mauritskade 21D, 1091 GC Amsterdam,
The Netherlands gpsr@mare-nostrum.co.uk

∞The paper used in this publication meets the minimum requirements of the
American National Standard for Information Sciences—
Permanence of Paper for Printed Library Materials, ANSI Z39.48-1992.

MARQUETTE UNIVERSITY PRESS
MILWAUKEE

for

Patrick W. Carey
who introduced me to and invited me into
the groundbreaking tradition of
graduate theological education for laywomen and -men
advanced by Marquette University

and

to the memory of

Shawnee Marie Daniels-Sykes, '07
(1960–2022)
whose holy life, boundless curiosity,
and brilliant theo-bioethical praxis
enfleshed that tradition

and

Robert M. Doran, S. J., '75
(1939–2021)
whose luminous and profound insight
into the human psyche, theology, and history
took Lonergan Studies to a cutting edge

Foreword

The 2025 Père Marquette Lecture in Theology is the fifty-fifth in a series commemorating the missions and explorations of Père Jacques Marquette, SJ (1637–75). This series of lectures was begun in 1969 under the auspices of the Marquette University Department of Theology. The Joseph A. Auchter Family Endowment Fund had endowed the lecture series. Joseph Auchter (1894–1986), a native of Milwaukee, was a banking and paper industry executive and a long-time supporter of education. The fund was established by his children as a memorial to him.

M. SHAWN COPELAND

M. Shawn Copeland is Professor Emerita of Systematic Theology, the Department of Theology, Boston College, Chestnut Hill, Massachusetts, and serves as theologian-in-residence at Saint Katharine Drexel Parish, Boston (Roxbury), Massachusetts. Professor Copeland is an internationally recognized Catholic theologian, scholar, and award-winning writer—the author and editor or co-editor of eight books, including *Enfleshing Freedom: Body, Race, and Being*, 2nd edition (Minneapolis: Fortress Press, 2023), which has been hailed as "a contemporary classic;" and (coed.) *Darkness, Desire, and Hope: Theology in a Time of Impasse, Engaging the Thought of Constance FitzGerald, OCD* (Collegeville, Minnesota: Liturgical Press, 2021). She also has published 150 articles, book chapters, and essays on spirituality, theological anthropology, political theology, social suffering, gender, and race and is recognized as one of the most important influences in North America in drawing attention to issues surrounding African American Catholics.

Born in Detroit, Michigan, Copeland earned the B.A. at Madonna College (now University), Livonia, Michigan in 1969 and the Ph.D. at Boston College, Chestnut Hill, Massachusetts, in 1991. From 1994 until 2002, Professor Copeland was a member of the Faculty of the Theology Department at Marquette. She held earlier academic appointments at Saint Norbert College (DePere, Wisconsin), Yale University Divinity School (New Haven, Connecticut), the Institute for Black Catholic Studies, Xavier University of Louisiana (New Orleans, Louisiana).

She has held visiting positions at Harvard Divinity School (Cambridge, Massachusetts), Emory University's Candler School of Theology (Atlanta, Georgia), and St. John's University (Queens, New York).

A former convener of the Black Catholic Theological Symposium (BCTS), a learned interdisciplinary society of Black Catholic scholars, Copeland was the first African American and first African American woman to be elected president of the Catholic Theological Society of America (CTSA). She served the American Academy of Religion (AAR) as co-chair of the Program Unit on Women and Religion, and as a member of the Steering Committees of the Black Theology Group and of the Womanist Approaches to Religion and Society Group.

Professor Copeland is the recipient of eight honorary degrees along with several awards for outstanding contributions to Catholic theology and Catholic intellectual life, including the College Theology Society's President's Award (2024), the John Courtney Murray Award, presented by the Catholic Theological Society of America (2018), and the Marianist Award, presented by the University of Dayton (2017).

Professor Copeland has lectured extensively in colleges, universities, seminaries, and divinity schools in the United States of America as well as in Australia, Belgium, Canada, France, Ireland, Italy, Kenya, Nigeria, Rwanda, Scotland, and South Africa. In

2019, she delivered both the Taylor Lectures at Yale University Divinity School and the Cunningham Lectures at New College, the University of Edinburgh, and during the 2020-2021 academic year, the McDonald Lectures at Candler School of Theology.

Acknowledgments

I thank Professor Cathal Doherty, S.J., the Père Marquette Lecture Committee, and the Faculty of Theology of Marquette University for inviting me to deliver the 2025 Lecture. I am humbled to be numbered among the outstanding group of theologians and scholars—some of whom have been my teachers—who have previously delivered this lecture.

The privilege of presenting this lecture provides me with the opportunity to visit with Marquette Theology Graduate Students and, in particular, to thank those students responsible for the "Lonergan on the Edge Conference," who have named an annual presentation in contextual theology in my honor. I also am very happy to be able to visit with this generation of Theology Department Faculty, some of whom are former students and fellow alumni of Boston College; and I am eager to renew my acquaintance with senior members of the Department, many of whom were my colleagues, nearly twenty years ago.

I am grateful to those who have read versions of this argument, especially Maureen Kondrick and Tyler Cosmer of Marquette University Press, who provided vital copy-editing assistance, and Barbara Bzura, whose keen eye for proof reading, astute questions, conversation, and financial knowledge and expertise inspired insights regarding commercial and transcendent value.

The Politics of Redemption:

The Doctrine, the Matter, the Law, and Grace

> With all wisdom and insight, [God] has made known to us the mystery of his will, according to his good pleasure that he set forth in Christ, as a plan (*oikonomia*) for the fullness of time, to gather up all things (*anakephalaiōsasthai*) in him, things in heaven and things on earth.
>
> (*Ephesians* 1: 9–10)[1]

The word 'redemption' carries a variety of meanings—incarnate and intersubjective, symbolic and cultural, religious and theological, political and economic, even ironic and contradictory. The English noun 'redemption' derives from the Latin

---

1 Biblical references are taken either from the *Jewish Study Bible* 2nd ed (Oxford / New York: Oxford University Press, 2014), Kindle, or *The New Greek / English Interlinear New Testament* (Carol Stream, IL: Tyndale House Publishers, 1990, 2020).

The designations 'African American' and 'Black' are used interchangeably to refer to descendants of the enslaved African peoples in the United States. The term 'African American' also may be applied to descendants of enslaved African peoples in Latin America (e.g., Brazil, Columbia,

redimere (*re-emere*) and the Old French reflexive verb *se rédimer* meaning 'to buy back'. Synonyms for the English verb 'redeem' range widely and include deliver, liberate, restore, retrieve, propitiate, save, vindicate.[2] Contemporary ordinary usage links the concept of redemption to finance and / or marketing (e.g., repayment of fixed-income securities or promotion of coupons or gift cards to be redeemed for goods or services).[3] Sociological and historical

---

Ecuador) and the Caribbean (e.g., Haiti, Cuba, Jamaica, Trinidad and Tobago). Within the United States, usage of this designation has been problematized by contemporary immigration from the African continent and the Caribbean. The words 'Black' and 'White' are capitalized when referring to *persons* or *groups*. The terms 'Indigenous,' 'Indian,' and 'Native' are used interchangeably with regard to the earliest inhabitants of North America (see, Roxanne Dunbar-Ortiz *An Indigenous Peoples' History of the United States, Revisioning History Book 3* (Boston: Beacon Press, 2015), Kindle.

2 See *New Oxford American Dictionary* and *Oxford American Writer's Thesaurus*, Microsoft online; also, Robert A. Dutch, ed., *The Original Roget's Thesaurus of English Words and Phrases* (New York: St. Martin's Press, 1965).

3 James Chen explains that the term "redemption" has different uses in the finance and business world. In finance, redemption refers to the repayment of any fixed-income security at or before the asset's maturity date. Bonds are the most common type of fixed-income security, but others include certificates of deposit (CDs), Treasury notes (T-notes), and preferred shares. Another use of the term "redemption" is in the context of coupons and gift cards which

studies associate redemption with ransom or buying back hostages, captives, or human beings who have been enslaved or trafficked. This latter specification of redemption as buying back those held captive or endangered was adapted by Christian teaching to explain theologically what Christ does for all humanity. Yet as Esther Reed insists:

> Redemption in its fullest and proper sense . . . is a doctrine which pertains to the destiny of the cosmos (Romans 8:19–24; Colossians 1:15–20) and challenges us to view all creation as called to give glory to God (Psalms 148; Isaiah 42:4, 43:19–21; Luke 19:40). God is God of both creation and redemption; there is no split in the divine economy. Indeed, writes Athanasius, the Word of God who filled all things everywhere at creation became incarnate in order that all things might be turned away from corruption and quickened by his presence: "no part of Creation is left void of Him: He has filled all things everywhere."[4]

---

consumers may redeem for products and services," in "Redemption: Definition in Finance and Business," https://www.investopedia.com/terms/r/redemption.asp (May 25, 2022).

4 Esther D. Reed, "Redemption," in *The Blackwell Companion to Modern Theology*, ed. Gareth Jones (Malden, MA: Blackwell Publishing, 2004), 228; see Athanasius, "Against the Heathen," in *The Nicene and Post-Nicene Fathers* 2nd series, Vol IV (Edinburgh: T. & T. Clark, 1989).

Redemption is one of several key beliefs that Christians have borrowed or coopted, reworked and appropriated from Judaism, the religion of Jesus (Yeshua) of Nazareth, whom Christians confess as the Christ of God.[5] The passage from the Letter to the Ephesians,[6] disputed authorship notwithstanding, sets out the elements of the Christian doctrine of redemption: "with all wisdom and insight [God] has made known to us the mystery of [the divine] will . . . set forth in Christ as a plan . . . to gather up all things in Christ, things in heaven and things on earth" (Ephesians 1:9–10). "The economy [*oikonomia*] is the actualization in time and history of the eternal plan of redemption, the providential ordering [*taxis*] of all things"[7] and their restoration [*anakephalaiôsis*] in Christ. Redemption is God's

---

5 For critiques of irresponsible Christian appropriation of the Jewish Scriptures, see Willie James Jennings, *The Christian Imagination: Theology and the Origins of Race* (Louisville: Westminster John Knox, 2010) and Wil Gafney, "Reading the Hebrew Bible Responsibly," in *The Africana Bible: Reading Israel's Scriptures from Africa and the African Diaspora*, ed. Hugh R. Page, Jr., et al. (Minneapolis: Fortress Press, 2010), especially, 47–48.

6 See E. Elizabeth Johnson, "Ephesians," in *Women's Bible Commentary* 3rd edition, ed. Carol A. Newsom, et al (Louisville: Westminster John Knox Press, 2012), 786.

7 Catherine Mowry LaCugna, *God for Us: The Trinity and Christian Life* (New York: HarperCollins Publishers, 1991), 25.

costly work of love through Christ in the power of the Holy Spirit: redeeming humankind for unity and identity as beloved of the Most High, and to communion with the Divine Transcendent Three; liberating, refreshing, enlivening; revitalizing, transforming, breathing new life into intersubjective relationships between and among humans (II Corinthians 3:18; II Peter 1:4); renewing, reviving, and healing the cosmos (Romans 8:21–23; Revelations 21:5). Reed succinctly captures three crucial aspects of redemption: "God's solidarity with humankind and especially those in need; deliverance from all that prevents life being lived to the full; and transformation from imperfection to perfection, from loss of potential to its fulfillment."[8]

We consider here God's loving, costly, gratuitous acts of redemption—solidarity, deliverance, and transformation—made known through divine revelation and "received on the Black frequency" in the situation of white racist supremacy in the United States of America.[9] Within the harrowing historical, religious, cultural, and social (i.e., political, economic, technological) context of nearly two hundred and fifty years of enslavement, God heard and answered the cries of enslaved Black

---

8 Reed, "Redemption," 227.

9 Olin P. Moyd, *Redemption in Black Theology* (Valley Forge, PA: Judson Press, 1979), 116.

people,[10] revealing the Divineself to them as God of the Enslaved. In kenotic solidarity, the eternal Word (*Logos / Sophia*) enfleshed blackness with and among the enslaved people; he became as they were—*no-person*, but chattel, an object of property to be bought and sold, used and abused; and he showed them his 'Way.' In solidarity, he was raped, whipped, brutalized, and lynched from a tree as they were; but the Black Messiah arose to life among them singing a wild, hope-filled blues song. The Black Messiah called out to the Spirit, who possessed the people—stirred them, moved them, animated them, radicalized them so that they might no longer serve the economy of a slave society, but "serve the truth of *God's economy*."[11]

To speak of redemption in this situation and in its aftermath foregrounds the "dangerous memory"[12] of the country's historical engagement in the

---

10 We should remember that the human persons who were kidnapped or captured in wars and sold by 'African' leaders or chiefs or kings to European slave traders did not consider themselves 'black.' These persons understood themselves as belonging to distinct religio-cultural linguistic groups such as the Ashanti or Fulani or Igbo or Yoruba, etc. Europeans, although often discerning distinctive cultural identities, called the enslaved captives by the color of their skin—black (*negro* in Spanish).

11 LaCugna, *God for Us*, 383. My italics.

12 Johann Baptist Metz, *Faith in History and Society*, trans. by J. Matthew Ashley (1977; New York: Crossroad Publishing, 1992), 66–67.

buying and selling, exploiting and profiting from Blackhuman flesh and the lingering residue of that sinful crime in ongoing social authorization and cultural tolerance of the subordination, segregation, neo-lynching, mass incarceration, surveillance, extra-judicial murder, victimization, and abuse of Blackhuman persons. Faithful and critical remembrance of such maldistributed, negative, enormous, vicious, transgenerational[13] humanly-engineered social oppression and the suffering it produced turns theology political and signifies how redemption is at stake in political theology.

Since this lecture ventures theology as political, let me clarify my usage of the word 'political.'[14] In my theological usage the word 'political' does *not* refer

---

13 William R. Jones, *Is God a White Racist? A Preamble to Black Theology* (1973; Boston: Beacon Press, 1998), 21–23. Jones identifies these characteristics of Black people's suffering and relates his account to that of Rabbi Richard Rubenstein, *After Auschwitz: Radical Theology and Contemporary Judaism* (New York: Bobbs-Merrill Press, 1966); see Beverly Eileen Mitchell, *Plantations and Death Camps: Religion, Ideology, and Human Dignity* (Minneapolis: Fortress, 2009).

14 The English word *political* derives from the ancient Greek word *polis*, which originally designated the administrative and religious center of a city, but in modern usage refers to an ancient Greek 'city-state' such as Athens or Sparta or Thebes. Plato's *Republic* is all about the political—how to order a *polis* so that citizens become just, learn and grow skilled in the practice of virtue, and together seek the common good. In the Platonic dialogues (especially the *Republic*),

to, signify, insinuate, or imply any particular partisan or pressure group, alliance or lobby, party or faction. In common parlance in the United States, we often refer to politics or the political in derisive or disparaging ways; and just as often we reduce politics or the political to transactional procedures of negotiating, brokering, dealing out, and delivering goods and / or services. Broadly construed, politics refers to "the activity through which people make, preserve, and amend the general rules under which they live."[15] I understand and appreciate politics as deeply related to our highest natural aspirations and values, rights and obligations, responsibilities and actions. Politics ought to evoke both a collective and individual, communal and personal desire to achieve and realize together a just and choiceworthy way of living through which together we, as people of good will, seek each one's flourishing and pursue the common human good.

---

    the standard for the common good is the virtuous life lived. The course of one's life is to be charted by seeking after, assenting to, and living in accordance with that which is reasonably most choiceworthy and worthwhile, with the flourishing of the potentialities of the human soul, namely, the virtues.

15 Andrew Heywood, "What Is Politics?" *Politics Review* 11, no. 2 (November 2001) *Gale General OneFile* (accessed October 14, 2024). https://link.gale.com/apps/doc/A80322532/ITOF?u=mlin_m_bostcoll&sid=bookmark-ITOF&xid=2e0e46d4

Christian theological reflection on the history of the cultural and social order of the United States with its breakdowns, mendacity, blindspots, and refusals to redress lingering injustices of expropriation, genocide, enslavement, gender and class oppressions and to rectify the corruption of freedom cannot but be political. Such reflection must kneel before the cross of the lynched Jesus of Nazareth in fidelity to the memory of his life, passion, death, and resurrection. Certainly, redemption can never be "an abstract soteriological concept."[16] Rather, this dangerous memory orders and directs us to active compassionate solidarity on behalf of the victims of history—the vanquished, forgotten dead. Christian political theological memory critically interrogates the structures of cultural and social power and rebukes our national amnesia. This necessarily political theology reproaches our casual forgetfulness of marginalized, repressed, dispossessed, enslaved bodies, admonishes our indifference to living black bodies, and "sharpens [our] social and political conscience in the interest of the suffering of others."[17]

The thirteen English colonies that became the United States of America included non-white persons *only reluctantly*. The Naturalization Act of

---

16 Joas Adiprasetya, "Johann Baptist Metz's *Memoria Passionis* and the Possibility of Forgiveness," *Political Theology* 18, no. 3 (May–June 2017): 237.

17 Metz, *Faith in History and Society*, 110.

1790 restricted U.S. citizenship to "any alien, being a free white person . . . of good character."[18] This legal definition tied U.S. citizenship to racial identity; from the earliest days of the nation, identity politics has shaped the electorate. Birthright citizenship or the right of citizenship for all individuals born within the country's territory regardless of parentage was not imagined as possible for non-white peoples.[19] Almost from the beginning, white racist supremacy saturated and continues to saturate the nation's putative Christian religious orientation, its cultural dispositions, and its social order.[20] This obdurate order refuses to recognize and to acknowledge the humanity and personhood of Black children, youth, women, and men, and continues to

---

18 U. S. Laws, Statutes, Etc. A bill to establish an uniform rule of naturalization, and to enable aliens to hold lands under certain restrictions. New York, Printed by Thomas Greenleaf. New York, 1790. Pdf. http://www.loc.gov/item/2020769535/

19 Three landmark court cases—*Yick Wo v. Hopkins* (1886), *United States v. Wong Kim Ark* (1898), *Takao Ozawa v. United States* (1922), and its parallel case *United States v. Bhagat Singh Thind* (1923)—illustrate the racialization of citizenship and contest the Chinese Exclusion Act of 1882, which was repealed only in 1943.

20 The Constitution of the United States prohibits the establishment of any one particular or state-approved religion, and the First Amendment of the Constitution allows for the free exercise of religion.

negate and obstruct the moral and social performance of being *Blackhuman-in-the-world*. So it is that in the United States, Blackhuman persons are artificially restricted and regulated in the struggle[21] to realize human dignity, exercise freedom, carry out mundane and ordinary activities, and live out a human and humane life.

The logic of authentic Blackhuman self-realization or performance of religious, communal, personal, cultural, and social freedom in service of living humanly and humanely through love and in hope correlates with a politics of redemption: this is the *field* of the lecture. I work this out in seven (7) *furrows*: the *first* probes the meanings of selected biblical passages of redemption in both the Hebrew Scriptures and in the Christian Scriptures or New Testament and considers pertinent theological interpretations of those passages; the *second* examines the trope of redemption in American colonial and antebellum history, religious thinking, and culture; the *third* considers Black people's encounter with and appropriation

---

21 We descendants of the enslaved Africans in the United States frequently use the word *struggle* to symbolize and signify our strenuous, transgenerational effort to wrest from God and religion, jurisprudence and legislation, culture and society freedom to live a dignified human and humane life. The struggle not only holds the nation accountable for its brazen defiance of its own ideals and laws, but also for its prolonged attachment to white racist supremacy and hetero-patriarchy.

of Christianity, particularly the Bible, in the context of chattel slavery; the *fourth* regards the matter, i.e., the fleshly, corporal bodies and material lives to be redeemed; the *fifth* treats the upending of Reconstruction or Black Redemption by the anger, resentment, and violence of those seeking the restoration of white racist dominance, that is, 'White Southern Redemption;' the *sixth* interrogates the supplanting of the reputed ideals of the Constitution of the United States and its laws through duplicity; the *seventh* theologizes Blackhuman living in the tragic subjunctive through grace; an *afterword* addresses what it means to enflesh struggle in our time.

I. Biblical and Theological Meanings of Redemption

The Hebrew words for 'redeemer,' 'redeem,' and 'redemption' derive from two roots, *pdh* [*pall* / *padha*] and *g'l* [*go'el* / *ga'al*], words that appear in the *Tanakh* (Hebrew Scriptures) at least 130 times, one-third of which are found in the Book of Isaiah. These words are used principally in relation to divine activity, but also may connote ordinary human affairs.[22] "Redemption," writes Donald D.

---

22 Donald Daniel Leslie asserts that "*G'l* is more restricted in usage and does not appear to have cognates in other Semitic languages. It is connected with family law and reflects the Israelite conception of the importance of preserving the

Leslie, means "salvation from the states or circumstances that destroy the value of human existence or human existence itself."[23] And Ingrid Maisch comments, "Salvation for the psalmist is deliverance from mortal danger, healing in sickness, liberation from captivity, ransom from slavery, help in a lawsuit, victory in battle, peace after political negotiations (Psalm 7:11; 18:28; 22:22; 34:7, 19f.; 55:17; 69:2; 86:2; 107:13, 19, 28, etc.)."[24]

---

solidarity of the clan. The *go'el* ("redeemer") is the next of kin who acts to maintain the vitality of his extended family group by preventing any breaches from occurring in it. Thus, he acquires the alienated property of his kinsman (Lev. 25:25) or purchases it when it is in danger of being lost to a stranger (cf. Jer. 32:6ff.). Possibly, too, he is required to support the widow of his next of kin in the event of her being dependent on this estate for her livelihood (cf. Ruth 4:4ff.). In any event, he redeems a clansman who has been reduced to slavery by poverty (Leviticus 25:47ff.) and avenges his blood when it has been shed (cf., e.g., Numbers 35:17–19)," "Redemption," in *Encyclopaedia Judaica*, 2nd ed., vol. 17, ed. Michael Berenbaum and Fred Skolnik (Detroit: Macmillan Reference USA, 2007), 151 https://link.gale.com/apps/doc/CX2587516544/GVRL.encyj?u=mlin_m_bostcoll&sid=bookmark-GVRL.encyj&xid=b186fb42.

23 Leslie, "Redemption," 151.

24 Ingrid Maisch, "Salvation—Biblical Concept," in *Sacramentum Mundi Online*, ed. Karl Rahner, et al (Leiden: Koninklijke Brill, 2016) doi: http://dx.doi.org/10.1163/2468-483X_smuo_COM_003942.

According to Leslie, when applied to divine activity, *padah* assumes the general meaning of deliverer, without involving the notion of payment or its equivalent. "God is, after all, the Lord of the universe and everything belongs to [God]."[25] The one place in Scripture, Leslie maintains, where such an exchange occurs is in Isaiah 43:3–4, and there the usage is rhetorical and *padah* is not employed:

> For I the LORD [ADONAI] am your God,
> The Holy One of Israel, your Savior.
> I give Egypt as a ransom for you,
> Ethiopia and Saba in exchange for you.
> Because you are precious to Me,
> And honored, and I love you,
> I give men in exchange for you
> And peoples in your stead (Isaiah 43:3–4).

"God's purpose," Leslie asserts, "is not to retain the right of possession, but to liberate people, both individuals and groups from their woes."[26] Redemption *from bondage* is cited in Deuteronomy 7:8: "It was because the LORD favored you and kept the oath He made to your fathers that the LORD freed you with a mighty hand and rescued [redeemed] you from the house of bondage, from the power of Pharaoh king of Egypt." Redemption from oppression is found in

---

25 Leslie, "Redemption," 151.
26 Leslie, "Redemption," 151.

Isaiah 1:27: "Zion shall be saved [redeemed] in the judgment; Her repentant ones in the retribution." Recall this verse from Deuteronomy 15:15: "Bear in mind that you were slaves in the land of Egypt and the LORD your God redeemed you. . . ."

In his study of the roots *pdh* [*padah*] and *g'l* [*go'el*], Olin Moyd adheres to Leslie's findings in showing that the terms 'redeemer,' 'redemption,' and 'redeem' are associated with

> the domain of commercial law [and] grew out of the sociocultural situation of the Hebrew tradition. . . . Most importantly, redemption in ancient Hebrew thought applied to salvation from woes, salvation from bondage, salvation from oppression, salvation from death, and salvation from other states and circumstances in the here and now.[27]

David Flusser presses the notion of redemption in the Talmud, which uses *padah* to refer to ransom or "the compensation required to avoid bodily punishment or to free oneself from an undesirable state or condition," and uses *ga'al* to mean redemption.[28] The sages of the Talmud, Flusser writes

> know nothing of a miraculous redemption of the soul by external means. There is no failing in man,

---

27 Moyd, *Redemption in Black Theology*, 43–44.
28 David L. Lieber, "Ransom," in *Encyclopaedia Judaica*, 2nd ed., 91–92.

whether collectively or as an individual, which requires special divine intervention and which cannot be remedied, with the guidance of the Torah, by man himself. As a result, the term *ge'ullah* is applied almost exclusively to national redemption, and became a synonym for national freedom. This idea of national freedom from subjection to other states is the main element in the yearnings of the people for the redemption of Israel, and it became even more pronounced during the period of Roman domination.[29]

Under Roman occupation, the term *ge'ullah* came to refer "almost exclusively to national redemption and became a synonym for national freedom." At the same time, the "image of a Messiah as redeemer" assumes a place of prominence, although he is "merely an instrument in the hands of God." The Messiah's role and action in redemption, like that of others such as Moses, serve a temporary function. The "final redemption will be accomplished by God Himself and will be eternal."[30]

---

29 Lieber, "Ransom," 91-92.

30 David Flusser, "Redemption," in *Encyclopaedia Judaica*, 2nd ed., 152. Flusser holds that a "quasi-transcendental and mystical element was introduced into the concept of redemption." Redemption was made to serve the "needs of the Most High," because "whenever [Israel] was exiled the Divine Presence was exiled with them." Thus, it is possible to say that "God *redeems* Himself with the redemption" (152).

"Redemption," Jon Levenson insists is "God's reparative, restorative, and triumphant intervention into the tragedy of fleshly, historical life."[31] Levison critiques any attempt to collapse redemption into individual ethical striving. Ancient Hebrew thought invested the notion of redemption (or salvation) with concrete meaning—redemption from oppression, from bondage, from grave danger or perilous circumstances; redemption (or salvation) for national liberation and freedom. Indeed, Levenson asserts: "The exodus has become a prototype of ultimate redemption, and historical liberation has become a partial proleptic experience of eschatological liberation, a token, perhaps *the* token of things to come."[32]

The Makers of the Spirituals and their descendants, including many contemporary Black theologians, took the substance of the exodus story (i.e., God's promise of emancipation and redemption, of favor and choice) as a prototype for their own yearning and struggle for emancipation, redemption, and freedom. Enslaved Black people took the *very God* who liberated the enslaved Hebrews as the God who would redeem *them* and *their descendants*. The

---

31 Jon Douglas Levenson, *Resurrection and the Restoration of Israel: The Ultimate Victory of the God of Life* (New Haven, CT: Yale University Press, 2006), 16.

32 Levenson, *Resurrection and the Restoration of Israel*, 27. Author's italics.

God of the Hebrews became their God. Indeed, the Makers of the Spirituals forged this classic expression of their confidence in that God who would surely vindicate them as they strained under "unmerited, involuntary, perpetual, absolute, and hereditary" bondage.[33]

> When Israel was in Egypt's land / Let my people go
> Oppressed so hard they could not stand / Let my people go
>
> Go down, Moses, / Way down in Egypt land
> Tell ole Pharaoh / To let my people go
>
> No more in bondage shall they toil / Let my people go
> Let them come out with Egypt's spoil / Let my people go

"It matters little to the oppressed who authored scripture," James Cone remarked; "what is important is whether it can serve as a weapon against oppressors."[34] Given the nature of the Spirituals, sacred black psalms, 'Go down, Moses' may not have been a weapon, but surely it served as both warning and proclamation.

---

33 Reverend David Barrow, *Involuntary, Unmerited, Perpetual, Absolute, Hereditary Slavery Examined; on the Principles of Nature, Reason, Justice, Policy and Scripture* (Lexington, KY, 1808), 14-15, 19, cited in David Brion Davis, *The Problem of Slavery in the Age of Revolution, 1770-1823* (Ithaca, NY and London: Cornell University Press, 1975), 555.

34 James H. Cone, *A Black Theology of Liberation* 50th Anniversary Edition (1970; Maryknoll, NY: Orbis Books, 2020), 33.

Womanist theologian Delores Williams questions the reliability of the testimony of the biblical witness to God's action on behalf of the redemption of enslaved Black people from bondage and oppression. Her questioning uncovers a "non-liberative strand"[35] woven in both the Hebrew and Christian Scriptures. Williams surveys several texts in the Hebrew Scriptures including Jeremiah 34:8–22 in which God commands that every Hebrew "should set free [their] Hebrew slaves, both male and female, and that no one should keep his fellow Judean enslaved." But she notes, "There is no mention of freedom for non-Jewish slaves."[36] The injunction in *Leviticus*, she implies, rejects enslavement of Hebrews, but accepts enslavement of males and females who may be acquired from among other peoples and nations.

> Such male and female slaves as you may have—it is from the nations round about you that you may acquire male and female slaves. You may also buy them from among the children of aliens resident among you, or from their families that are among you, whom they begot in your land. These shall become your property: you may keep them as

---

35 Delores S. Williams, *Sisters in the Wilderness: The Challenge of Womanist God-Talk* (Maryknoll, NY: Orbis Books, 1993), 144, 147.

36 Williams, *Sisters in the Wilderness*, 146.

> possession for your children after you, for them to inherit as property for all time. Such you may treat as slaves. But as for your Israelite kinsmen, no one shall rule ruthlessly over the other. (Leviticus 25: 44–46)

Taking what she calls a "non-Hebrew perspective," Williams finds "no clear indication that God is against the perpetual enslavement" of non-Hebrews. "One wonders," she asks, "how biblically derived messages of liberation can be taken seriously by today's masses of poor, homeless African Americans, female and male, who consider themselves to be experiencing a form of slavery—economic enslavement by the capitalistic American economy."[37]

Williams reproves black theology's use of the exodus story as paradigmatic for interpreting black experience. Such usage she asserts is too often methodologically uncritical, potentially self-serving, and over-identified with biblical Israel. These shortcomings threaten existential vitality and formation of critical social consciousness in the African American Christian community. She calls Black theologians to periodize or historically contextualize the differing functional usages of the exodus story within black religious, cultural, and political life (e.g., the period of enslavement, Emancipation, Reconstruction, the Civil Rights Era, and so on).

---

37 Williams, *Sisters in the Wilderness*, 146–147.

The Politics of Redemption

Williams advances a "womanist hermeneutic of identification-ascertainment," a hermeneutic that allows Black theologians to identify and understand at what points the biblical text itself must be critically and rigorously interrogated, especially "those instances where the text supports oppression, exclusion and even death of innocent people."[38] Moreover, she throws a spotlight on textual references to the abuse, depersonalization, and devaluation of enslaved women, particularly "non-Hebrew female slaves, especially those of African descent, are not on equal terms with the Hebrews and are not woven into this biblical story of election and exodus."[39] Williams demands that black theology no longer accommodate itself uncritically to the Bible, but accommodate the Bible to the urgent necessities of the blacklife world.[40] From a womanist perspective, redemption is not and can never be *merely immaterial*.

The New Testament uses the Greek term *sótéria* (salvation) to refer both to bodily well-being and to the state or condition of spiritual life. "The word salvation," writes Maisch, "is a religious term and is almost never applied to purely earthly conditions."[41]

---

38 Williams, *Sisters in the Wilderness*, 150.

39 Williams, *Sisters in the Wilderness*, 147; see Exodus 21:1–11; Leviticus 19: 20–22.

40 Williams, *Sisters in the Wilderness*, 4.

41 Maisch, "Salvation—Biblical Concept," in *Sacramentum Mundi Online*.

Even if the word is used to advert to bodily healing or physical help or rescue from grave danger, always "it points to a profounder reality because of its connection with faith."[42] The Apostle Paul articulates salvation as rooted in faithful identification with Christ's death and resurrection, as "a provisional transformation in the power of the Spirit in anticipation of our own death and resurrection."[43] We make that identification vivid in efforts to live a life according to the Spirit. Paul challenges: "Work out your salvation with fear and trembling, because it is God who works in you both to will and to succeed" (Phil 2:12f; 3:13f).

But, when writing of redemption or salvation, Paul frequently deploys the language of slavery with its polarities of slavery / freedom, slave / master. In fact, the word slave (*dulos*) appears in the New Testament at least 130 times and 31 times in key Pauline letters.[44] Slaveholding was part of the

---

42 Maisch, "Salvation—Biblical Concept," in *Sacramentum Mundi Online*.

43 Klaus Nürnberger, "Paul's Concept of Salvation–Culmination of an Evolutionary Process," *Scriptura* 80 (2002): 236.

44 The word 'slave' appears in Romans ten times, in 1 Corinthians five times, in 2 Corinthians two times, in Galatians eleven times, in Ephesians three times, in Colossians three times, and once in both Philippians and Philemon. Modern scholarship points to differences in literary style, vocabulary, and theology to dispute the Pauline authenticity of sections of Colossians and Ephesians along with 2 Thessalonians.

fabric of the ancient world and was premised on control and honor. In his analysis of ancient slaveholding societies, sociologist Orlando Patterson notes that

> the slave was considered a degraded person; the honor of the master was enhanced by the subjection of his slave; and wherever slavery became structurally very important, the whole tone of the slaveholders' culture tended to be highly honorific.[45]

Clarice Martin in "The *Haustafeln* (Household Codes) in African American Biblical Interpretation: 'Free Slaves' and 'Subordinate Women,'" qualifies her discussion: "First, by *Haustafeln* I mean the more complete domestic codes in Colossians 3:18-4:1; Ephesians 5:21-6:9, and 1 Peter 2:18–3:7, where the *Haustafeln* genre is most explicit. I exclude 1 Timothy 2:8–15; 5:1–2; 6:1–2; Titus 2:1–10; 3:1. Second, it is my position that the *Haustafeln* and letters in which they are found are not Pauline, but Deutero-Pauline. The question of whether the *Haustafeln* are Pauline is, of course, linked to the question of the authenticity of Colossians, Ephesians, and 1 Peter. I would argue that Colossians and Ephesians are Deutero-Pauline— that is, written by circles of Paul's students on the model of the Pauline letter, and that 1 Peter is pseudonymous," *Stony the Road We Trod: African American Biblical Interpretation* 30th Anniversary Expanded Edition, ed., Cain Hope Felder (Minneapolis: Fortress Press, 2021), 119 of 352, Kindle.

45 Orlando Patterson, *Slavery and Social Death, A Comparative Study* (Cambridge, MA and London: Harvard University Press, 1982), 79.

Moreover, in antiquity "the abolition of slavery was intellectually inconceivable, and socially, politically and economically impossible."[46] But it is well to remember that no particular race or skin color was fixed to slavery or became isomorphic with it. Sheila Briggs in a commentary on Paul's Letter to the Galatians states:

> One may argue that Paul's use of the language of slavery in figurative speech did not constitute an endorsement of slavery in the social realm; however, one cannot simply sever the rhetorical strategy from the content of discourse. Certainly, Paul was not addressing here the social institution of slavery, but the distinctions that ancient slavery made between person and person, between human group and human group, are perpetuated here, even if not in their original social form.[47]

"At times," writes Mitzi J. Smith, "Paul seems unable to empathize with the slave's socially and physically annihilating condition. For example, Paul arguably advises slaves and circumcised or uncircumcised men to be content with their present state (1 Cor

---

46 Patterson, "Paul, Slavery and Freedom: Personal and Socio-Historical Reflections," *Semeia* 83/84 (2004): 266.

47 Sheila Briggs, "Galatians," in *Searching the Scriptures: A Feminist Commentary*, vol. 2, ed. Elisabeth Schüssler Fiorenza (New York: The Crossroad Publishing Company, 1994), 224.

The Politics of Redemption

7:21)."[48] Paul also seems to overlook the fact that Jesus died a dishonorable death—one reserved for seditionists and rebellious slaves.

Jesus admonished his followers to become slaves to all: "Whoever wishes to become great among you must be your servant, and whoever wishes to be first among you must be slave of all" (Mark 10:43–45). According to Jennifer Glancy, "this saying stands out for its implicit challenge to the ethos of slaveholding."[49] This instruction is not included in John's Gospel, but Jesus *performed* it: He washed the feet of the disciples gathered for the Passover meal (John 13: 3–11). In the ancient world, as a gesture of hospitality and kindness, wealthy householders welcomed guests by having a low-ranking female slave wash their feet. Householders who did not possess slaves assigned this duty to one of the women. The Jesus in the Fourth Gospel "defies the hierarchical and gender norms of his day," enfleshes what it means to be

---

[48] Mitzi J. Smith, "Slavery in the Early Church," in *True to Our Native Land: An African American New Testament Commentary*, ed. Brian K. Blount (Minneapolis: Fortress Press, 2007), 11.

[49] Compare Matthew 20:26–27, Luke 22:26. Glancy explains that "Jews and pagans in the ancient world sometimes styled themselves as 'slaves of God' or 'slaves of [some god].' . . . Such appellations advanced the status of the person so named. Not so with the designation 'slave of all,'" in her *Slavery as a Moral Problem in the Early Church and Today* (Minneapolis: Fortress Press, 2011), 24.

a slave of all.⁵⁰ Clarice Martin comments: "The child and the slave who are typically relegated to the lowest rung of the patriarchal household ladder become, in the ministry of Jesus, a primary paradigm for authentic discipleship."⁵¹ But, no early Christian community required or demanded slaveholders to manumit or free enslaved persons as a condition for their baptism.⁵² Rather, Paul's Letters to the Colossians (3:22–25) and to the Ephesians (6:5–8), repeat the regulation: "Slaves be submissive to your masters."⁵³ Perhaps, the increased participation of women and enslaved persons in the Jesus movement unnerved and disrupted the order of the patriarchal household. The household codes, Martin contends, functioned "to reinforce and secure 'proper household management,' and thus conformity to generally accepted societal norms. Such conformity would minimize the perception that the Christians were a threat to the Greco-Roman social

---

50 Glancy, *Slavery as a Moral Problem in the Early Church and Today*, 24.

51 Martin, "The *Haustafeln* (Household Codes)," 233 of 352, Kindle.

52 Glancy declares "It is an interesting thought experiment to ponder how differently Christianity might have developed if early Christian communities had made freeing one's slaves a precondition of baptism," *Slavery as a Moral Problem in the Early Church and Today*, 24–25.

53 Martin, "The *Haustafeln* (Household Codes) in African American Biblical Interpretation," 233 of 352.

order."⁵⁴ Hence, women and enslaved persons were coerced to submit to the societal and patriarchal ordering of the status-quo.⁵⁵

Williams observes that one might agree with Cone and other Black liberation theologians that Jesus was thinking of the liberation of the oppressed when reportedly (Luke 4:18–19) he preached from the Scroll of the prophet Isaiah (61:1–2) in his hometown synagogue. But she questions what Jesus could have had in mind with these instructions to the twelve: "Go nowhere among the Gentiles, and enter no town of the Samaritans, but go rather to the lost sheep of the house of Israel" (Matthew 10:5–6). For Williams this instruction "suggests a kind of bias against the non-Jew that accords well with Paul's way of situating Hagar, the female slave, and her progeny outside the promise of freedom he describes in Galatians 5."⁵⁶

---

54 Martin, "The *Haustafeln* (Household Codes) in African American Biblical Interpretation," 233 of 352.

55 For more than two thousand years, Christianity—Catholic and Protestant—in too many of its official documents, theological statements, ritual and social actions has continued to restrict some Baptized members from certain rites, sacraments, and offices (e.g., the exclusion of women from presbyteral ordination) and too often to exclude or dissuade some persons (e.g., LGBTQI+, people of color) from active participation. Christianity—Catholic and Protestant—too often has muffled opposition by Christians to the civil and political order.

56 Williams, *Sisters in the Wilderness*, 147.

Further, Williams contests "the way in which many Christians, including black women, have been taught to image redemption."[57] Christian churches including African American denominational churches[58] teach and preach redemption (or salvation) as occurring through Jesus' death on the cross in atonement for our sin. But, in sexist or misogynist, racist and heterosexist contexts, such traditional and orthodox theological interpretation too often endorses a 'suffering Jesus' as a model for women, in particular for Blackwomen and women of color. These women along with LGBTQI+ persons and other persons of color are coached and coaxed to a pseudo-humility of invisibility, suffering, silence and submission when confronted with socially constructed oppression (Philippians 2:8). These persons are urged to imitate a 'suffering Jesus' who has become the "ultimate surrogate figure."[59] Theologically analyzing the feminicide in Cuidad Juárez, Nancy Pineda-Madrid agrees:

---

57 Williams, *Sisters in the Wilderness*, 161.

58 Williams distinguishes "between the black church as invisible and rooted in the soul of community memory and the African American denominational churches as visible. Contrary to the nomenclature in current black theological, historical and sociological works, in this book *the black church* is not used to name both the invisible black church and the African American denominational churches," *Sisters in the Wilderness*, 206.

59 Williams, *Sisters in the Wilderness*, 162.

The Politics of Redemption

> When the dominant forces of society reduce Jesus' redemptive significance to his suffering and sacrifice, then suffering and sacrifice in turn function as the central means by which women finally obtain redemption. Suffering and sacrifice are held up as unambiguously good. Accordingly, women and those who are economically poor end up having to make the greatest sacrifices in order to realize their salvation.[60]

So it is that *all* women and those who are marginalized in any society are dosed with the ideology of sacrifice and suffering.

"Can there be salvific power for black women," Williams asks, "in Christian images of oppression meant to teach something about redemption?"[61] Womanist theologians, she insists, must demonstrate to black women "that their salvation does not depend upon any form of surrogacy made sacred by traditional or orthodox understandings of Jesus' life and death."[62] Rather Williams maintains that "The resurrection of Jesus and the kingdom of God theme in Jesus' ministerial vision provide black women with the knowledge that God has, through

---

60 Nancy Pineda-Madrid, *Suffering and Salvation in Ciudad Juárez* (Minneapolis: Augsburg Fortress Publishers, 2011), 90.

61 Williams, *Sisters in the Wilderness*, 162.

62 Williams, *Sisters in the Wilderness*, 164.

Jesus, shown humankind how to live peacefully, productively and abundantly in relationship."[63] His vision and praxis are ethical in word and deed, curative and reparative, restorative and cleansing, prayerful and compassionate. By focusing on Jesus' life-giving ministry, womanist theologians "show black women that God did not intend the surrogacy roles they have been forced to perform. God did not intend the defilement of their bodies."[64] Williams concludes forcefully:

> Humankind is redeemed through Jesus' ministerial vision and life and not through his death. There is nothing divine in the blood of the cross. God does not intend black women's surrogacy experience. Neither can Christian faith affirm such an idea. Jesus did not come to be a surrogate. Jesus came for life.[65]

Williams neither forgets nor ignores the cross of the crucified Jesus and the massive suffering and humiliation that ignominious death brought about; at the same time, she urges black women not to glorify the cross or suffering. "To do so," she asserts, "is to render [Black women's] exploitation sacred. To do so is to glorify the sin of defilement."[66]

---

63 Williams, *Sisters in the Wilderness*, 167.

64 Williams, *Sisters in the Wilderness*, 166.

65 Williams, *Sisters in the Wilderness*, 167.

66 Williams, *Sisters in the Wilderness*, 167.

Klaus Nürnberger holds that Paul's theology is "predominantly eschatological theology."[67] Further, he maintains: "Baptism symbolises the integration of a believer into a new eschatological reality which finds provisional but concrete expression in the community of believers. The Spirit replaces the law as the boundary mark of the new community."[68] Such a theology accentuates the call of an individual to faith and conversion, to baptism and commitment to living the 'way' Jesus taught. The prominence of the eschatological may serve to discourage agitation for the re-arrangement or dismantling of oppressive social structures. The eschatological may signify the 'other-worldly,' but even interpretations of 'realized' eschatology depend upon potentialities of a *future-yet-to-come*. And, that *future-yet-to-come* must anticipate outcomes of concrete exercises of asymmetrical power dynamics in the here-and-now.

Paul exhorts slaves to

> obey your earthly masters with fear and trembling, in singleness of heart, as you obey Christ; not only while being watched, and in order to please them, but as slaves of Christ. . . . And

---

67 Nürnberger, "Paul's Concept of Salvation–Culmination of an Evolutionary Process," 235.

68 Nürnberger, "Paul's Concept of Salvation–Culmination of an Evolutionary Process," 240.

> masters, do the same to them. Stop threatening, for you know that both of you have the same Master in heaven, and with him there is no partiality. (Ephesians 6: 5, 9)

This enjoinder foregrounds shared spiritual equality before God even as it obscures, although does not erase, the asymmetrical power dynamics (i.e., psychic, cultural, physical, gender / sexual, social, and legal) between master and slave. This instruction departs from, opposes the teaching of the Hebrew Scriptures which did not separate redemption from the brutal conditions of bondage or enslavement. Redemption, with its "grammar" of *deliverance from* or *buying back*, accentuated the anxiety, oppressive social suffering, and materiality of those conditions.[69] In affirming the spiritual equality of masters and slaves, Pauline injunctions allowed, indeed, even encouraged Christian theology and preaching during the more than two-hundred-year period of enslavement in the United States to emphasize and amplify the spiritualization of redemption or salvation. This intensification rendered the brutal and brutalizing psychic, cultural, physical, gender / sexual, social, and legal conditions of slavery *immaterial*—except in the minds

---

69 George Shulman, *American Prophecy: Race and Redemption in American Political Culture* (Minneapolis: University of Minnesota Press, 2008), 259n14.

and hearts of Blackhuman persons whose very bodies and lives were made *material*.

II. Redemption in American Colonial and Antebellum History, Religious Thinking, and Culture

From the colonial era forward, the notion of redemption has functioned as a "troubling," "powerful trope,"[70] permeating America's history, religious thinking, racialized political culture, and achievement of freedom. At the same time, for enslaved Africans and their descendants, collectively and individually, redemption was weighted with material, cultural, and religious meanings even as it was complexified by and entwined with commercial and transcendent value. This two-part section calls attention to statutory, literal, and religious appeals of settler-colonists and of enslaved Africans to redemption.

§ Only rarely, do we citizens of the United States engage our colonial heritage; when we do, we romanticize that heritage. Such romanticizing conceals complex motives, self-serving decision-making,

---

70 Carole Emberton, *Beyond Redemption: Race, Violence, and the American South after the Civil War* (Chicago and London: University of Chicago Press, 2013), 2 of 286, 3 of 286, Kindle.

and violence. That romanticizing glosses over the invasion, disruption, and near extinction of Indigenous peoples and the practice of enslaving Africans. Indeed, prior to European contact

> an estimated 5 million people lived in what is now the continental United States [but] by 1900, 95 percent of the precontact population had been wiped out by European-borne diseases, war, forced relocation, forced labor, dietary changes, and other causes related to European colonialism.[71]

That invasion and usurpation of land was supported by the European claim of dominion over the so-called 'new world' as "fruits of discovery." England's Henry VII secured claim to North America based on John Cabot's explorations between 1497 and 1498.[72] These claims were validated and

---

71 Jim Wallis, *America's Original Sin: Racism, White Privilege, and the Bridge to a New America* (Grand Rapids, MI: Brazos Press, 2016), 39; see, Dunbar-Ortiz, *An Indigenous Peoples' History of the United States*, especially chapter 1, and Seth Davis, "American Colonialism and Constitutional Redemption," *California Law Review* 105, no. 6 (December 2017): 1751–1806.

72 Adam Dahl, *Slavery and the Empire of Free Soil: Settler Colonialism and the Foundations of Modern Democratic Thought* (Lawrence: University Press of Kansas, 2018), 134; see John L. Allen, "From Cabot to Cartier: The Early Exploration of Eastern North America, 1497–1543," *Annals of the Association of American Geographer* 82, no. 3 (September 1992): 500–21.

affirmed in a series of papal bulls or official papal decrees that accorded Catholic rulers the right to

---

The Eleventh Session of the United Nations Permanent Forum on Indigenous Issues (UNPFII) was devoted to the Doctrine of Discovery. See Robert J. Miller, et al., *Discovering Indigenous Lands: The Doctrine of Discovery in the English Colonies* (New York: Oxford University Press, 2010): "On 13 September 2007, the United Nations General Assembly adopted the long-anticipated Declaration on the Rights of Indigenous Peoples by a vote of 143:4. The UN Declaration was drafted negotiated, and advocated for by Indigenous peoples from dozens of countries for more than 20 years before it was finally adopted. The only four countries that voted against the Declaration were Australia, Canada, New Zealand, and the United Sates" (Miller et al., 'The Doctrine of Discovery,' *Discovering Indigenous Lands: The Doctrine of Discovery in the English Colonies* [Oxford, 2010; online edition, Oxford Academic, 1 Sept. 2010), https://doi.org/10.1093/acprof:oso/9780199579815.003.0001]) and Andrew Boyd, "Papal Condemnation of the Doctrine of Discovery," *Church Life Journal* (August 30, 2022), https://churchlifejournal.nd.edu/articles/papal-condemnation-of-the-doctrine-of-discovery/#_ftnref13. Boyd writes: "Neither of the bulls of Nicholas concerned the Americas nor the treatment of indigenous peoples. In the moral theology of the time, there was only one form of justified slavery, the capture and indenture of belligerents as prisoners of war, and then only during a just war. Further, these were practical decisions delimited by time and circumstance, not universal moral declarations."

subdue and subjugate *non-Christians* and take possession of their lands.[73]

More than a century later, the English continued to appeal to principles derived from these decrees to bolster their claims to legitimate jurisdiction over a territory and its people including "first discovery, sustained possession, voluntary self-subjection by the native peoples, and armed conquest successfully maintained."[74] English settler-colonists assumed North America to be a *terra nullius*, a land belonging to no

---

73 The 'doctrine of discovery' may be traced through a series of papal bulls or edicts, including *Dum Diversas* (1452) by Pope Nicholas V, *Inter Caetera* (1493) by Pope Alexander VI. Roughly thirteen months later, *Inter Caetera* was abrogated by the *Treaty of Tordesillas* (1494) that settled ongoing disputes between Spain and Portugal. Andrew Boyd maintains that the papal bull "was concerned with Christian evangelization," while the *Treaty of Tordesillas* "with discovery, colonization, and wealth [and thus] better acknowledged as the genesis of the doctrine of discovery," "Papal Condemnation of the Doctrine of Discovery," *Church Life Journal* (August 30, 2022), https://churchlifejournal.nd.edu/articles/papal-condemnation-of-the-doctrine-of-discovery/#_ftnref13. See Mark Charles, Soong-Chan Rah, *Unsettling Truths: The Ongoing, Dehumanizing Legacy of the Doctrine of Discovery* (Downers Grove, IL: Intervarsity Press, 2019), 14 of 237, Kindle; Vine Deloria Jr., ed., *Of Utmost Good Faith* (New York: Bantam Books, 1971), 6–39.

74 Francis Jennings, *The Invasion of America: Indians, Colonialism, and the Cant of Conquest* (New York: W. W. Norton & Company, 1975), 105.

The Politics of Redemption

one; but they found an inhabited land, "a humanized landscape almost everywhere," as William Denevan put it.[75] Settler-colonists not only claimed the land but also claimed the Indigenous peoples as their subjects and asserted rule. Not surprisingly, Indigenous peoples resisted and declared that they were entitled to govern themselves. If initially, the Indigenous peoples were open, hospitable, and helpful, they soon grew wary. Soldiers and merchants kidnapped several Indians—transporting them to England, even selling some as slaves to the Spanish.[76]

The English settler-colonists known to us as Puritans arrived in 'New' England in 1630, roughly a decade after their Pilgrim counterparts. The terms 'Pilgrims' and 'Puritans,' even in scholarship, sometimes are conflated and used inaccurately: Pilgrims held themselves to be separatists, Puritans considered themselves reformers. Both groups understood themselves as thoroughly English, subject to English law, loyal

---

75 William M. Denevan, "The Pristine Myth: The Landscape of the Americas in 1492," *Annals of the Association of American Geographers* 82, no. 3 (September 1992): 369.

76 See James E. Seelye et al., ed., *Shaping North America: From Exploration to the American Revolution* (Santa Barbara, CA and Denver: ABC-CLIO, LLC, 2018); James Rosier, *A True Relation of the Most Prosperous Voyage Made this Present Year 1605, by Captain George Weymouth in the Discovery of the Land of Virginia* (London: Eliot's Court Press, 1605). Weymouth kidnapped several members of an Indian hunting party and transported them to England.

to the English sovereign. Further, both Pilgrims and Puritans were religious dissenters seeking relief from interference with their spirituality and religious lives, and their interpretations of the polity and theology of the Church of England. Both groups believed in the right to worship according to conscience and to carry out their interpretations of biblically-based Christian living without outside interference; both groups were deeply influenced by the theology of John Calvin.[77]

The Puritan worldview as reconstructed from extant sermons, tracts, theological works, letters, diaries, journals, and personal conversion stories has preoccupied the American imagination, and redemption figured prominently in that worldview. Puritans made the dangerous ocean voyage "to establish a new 'Holy Commonwealth' in North America. They considered America their Promised Land, thus taking biblical scripture as prophecy and anticipating its fulfillment in their own lived reality in North America."[78] Lay preacher and lawyer John Winthrop, their leader, had a vision of communal life in this promised land held together by a kind of

---

77 R. Ward Holder, "Calvin's Heritage," in *The Cambridge Companion to John Calvin*, ed. Donald K. McKim (2004; Cambridge: Cambridge University Press, 2006), 251 https://doi.org/10.1017/CCOL0521816475

78 Heike Paul, *The Myths That Made America: An Introduction to American Studies* (Bielefeld, Germany: Transcript Verlag, 2014), 138 https://www.jstor.org/stable/j.ctv1wxsdq. Paul makes this clarification: "New England Puritanism

"social contract," an organism "knit together in this worke as one man [sic] . . . [aiming] to partake of each other's strength and infirmity, joy and sorrow, weal and woe. . . . The care of the public must oversway all private respects.'"[79]

The settler-colonists quite quickly became involved in economic affairs that allowed them, with initial assistance from Indigenous peoples then the labor of enslaved Africans, to extract wealth from the resources of the colony, thus enriching themselves and the colonizing power—England. "The Massachusetts Bay and Plymouth colonies statutorily sanctioned slavery as part of the 1641 Body of Liberties," three years after Africans arrived.[80] The

---

was not homogeneous though and cannot be interpreted monolithically; in fact, the experience of 'America' crucially transformed the Puritan religious dogma and increasingly led to conflicts among the Puritans about what their Promised Land should look like," *The Myths That Made America*, 150. The Puritans' basic Calvinistic religious beliefs may be summarized in the acronym TULIP: total depravity, unconditional election, limited atonement, irresistible grace, and perseverance of the saints.

79 John Winthrop, *The Winthrop Papers* (Boston: Massachusetts Historical Society, 1931), 295, cited in Paul, *The Myths That Made America*, 152, 153. This may allude to Romans 12: 4-8 and Ephesians 4:16.

80 In 1640, Colonial Virginia punished three runaway indentured servants: for the White servants the time of their indenture was increased, but the Black servant, John Punch was sentenced to perpetual servitude.

Body of Liberties outlawed "bond slavery, villenage, or captivity" among the White settler-colonists, unless they were lawful captives taken in just wars and, "such strangers as willfully sell themselves or are sold to us" to be held in slavery according to "the law of God established in Israell [sic] concerning such persons."[81] Historians find it difficult to determine why slavery developed in the New England colonies, since there was no large crop that required an extensive labor force. Reportedly, in 1700, Black people "numbered less than a thousand and were never more than 3 percent of the population."[82]

White Puritans took keen notice of the difference in skin color between and among the Indigenous peoples and the enslaved Africans. They sought to dominate and control Indigenous peoples and Africans—suppressing their agency, disciplining them, renaming them, selecting marriage partners for them, controlling their movements, hiring them out, preventing Indigenous and African peoples from owning firearms. Verbal, emotional, and physical abuse of Indigenous and African peoples was common, and White New Englanders exercised authority over them to demonstrate and reinforce white racial superiority.

---

81 A. Leon Higginbotham, Jr., *In the Matter of Color: Race and the American Legal Process: The Colonial Period* (New York: Oxford University Press, 1980), 61–62.

82 Higginbotham, *In the Matter of Color*, 71.

Puritan clergy and laity pressed theological meanings of redemption to explain social realities. Cotton Mather, a prominent minister, theologian, and slaveholder, held that slavery was "morally redemptive."[83] When the English Crown threatened to revoke the charter of the Massachusetts Bay Colony, Mather "made an almost desperate plea for the preservation of the 'New England Way,' reiterating once more the role of the colony in a global scheme of redemption and salvation."[84] White clergy and laity sought "to deliver themselves, their distinctly puritan society (including the institution of race-based slavery), and blacks and Indians from problems their ordering of colonial New England had created."[85]

---

83 Herbert Robinson Marbury, *Pillars of Cloud and Fire: The Politics of Exodus in African American Biblical Interpretation* (New York: New York University Press, 2015), 31.

84 Paul, *The Myths That Made America*, 159. Winthrop had a key role in shaping and founding the Massachusetts Bay Colony and served 18 annual terms as Governor. Works that treat the significance of 'redemption' in the Puritan worldview include Perry Miller, *The New England Mind: The Seventeenth Century* (Cambridge, MA.: Harvard University Press, 1954), idem., *The New England Mind: From Colony to Province* (Cambridge, MA: Harvard University Press, 1953); and Harry S. Stout, *The New England Soul: Preaching and Religious Culture in Colonial New England* (New York: Oxford University Press, 1986).

85 Richard Bailey, *Race and Redemption in Puritan New England* (Oxford: Oxford University Press, 2011), 115.

Gradually, some White New Englanders grew uncomfortable with the institution of slavery and "developed a sense of moral dis-ease, seen most clearly in their attempts to redeem the contradictions of their society."[86] Yet the Puritans maintained that their 'city on a hill' should include slavery, which they considered "a social good"[87] that held a vital role in God's plan of redemption. "White New Englanders," Bailey concludes, "neglected to recognize, however, that as they strived for redemption, they all too often created raced identities that denigrated and racialized the very persons they hoped to redeem."[88]

§ Redemption features significantly in the religio-cultural world created by enslaved Africans. Here their struggle for redemption and freedom from perpetual bondage takes center stage. Redemption required enslaved persons to strategically understand the commercial value of a 'slave.' "Between 1820 and 1860," Walter Johnson contends, "the slave trade—urban and rural—accounted for a significant portion of the South's economy. . . . As [enslaved Black] people passed through the trade, representing something close to half a billion dollars in property, they spread wealth wherever they

---

86 Bailey, *Race and Redemption in Puritan New England*, 114.

87 Marbury, *Pillars of Cloud and Fire*, 46.

88 Bailey, *Race and Redemption in Puritan New England*, 114.

went."[89] With chilling and poignant precision, he remarks: "Slavery reduced a person [to] a price."[90] Johnson records "the list of names, numbers, and outcomes double-entered" in the *Slave Record* kept by Mississippi River trader John White. Here are some of the human chattel in White's entries:

Cynthia Branham, 23, $515.00
   Sold to McRae through Coffman, $687.75

Isabel Evans, 17, $600.00
   Sold to Mr. Herne, cash $750.00

William Robards, 24, $750.00
   Sold to C. H. Harris, N. Orleans, $875.00

Joe Fields, 21, $715.00
   Sold to Etienne Landry, Lafourche, cash $800.00[91]

Redemption also demanded that enslaved persons perceive their transcendent value, the inherent worth and dignity of their personhood, their creation in the indelible image and likeness of God, their powers of reason, self-consciousness, and self-reflection, their capacity to form and sustain, enjoy and refrain from relationships. "The value of a slave as property," writes Arnold Sio, "resides in

---

89 Walter Johnson, *Soul by Soul: Life inside the Antebellum Slave Market* (Cambridge, MA and London: Harvard University Press, 1999), 6.

90 Johnson, *Soul by Soul*, 2.

91 Johnson, *Soul by Soul*, 45.

his being a person, but his value as a person rests in his status being defined as property."[92] Formerly enslaved Tom Windham, interviewed at the age of 98, precisely grasped the transcendent value of enslaved people when he said: "I think we should have our liberty cause us ain't hogs or horses—us is human flesh."[93] Chattel slavery produced "ontologically discordant beings."[94]

Redemption materialized in multiple, anticipatory, often ingenious forms; achieving it required negotiating skill, raw nerve, and fortitude. Consider that Venture Smith at the age of 31 made a down payment on his own redemption from slavery. Valued as property, he was unable to enter into a formal contract, but a freed Black man stood security for him. When not engaged in work assigned him by slaveholder Colonel Oliver Smith, Venture planted and sold produce, hired himself out as a wood cutter, and harvested

---

92 Arnold A. Sio, "Interpretations of Slavery: The Slave Status in the Americas," *Comparative Studies in Society and History* 7, no.3 (April 1965): 300.

93 Tom Windham, Interview by Beatrice Bowden, *Slave Narratives: A Folk History of Slavery in the United States from Interviews with Former Slaves*, vol. II: *Arkansas Narratives*, edited by Federal Writers' Project of the Works Progress Administration (Washington, D.C.: Library of Congress, 1937), cited in R. A. Judy, *Sentient Flesh: Thinking in Disorder, Poiesis in Black* (Durham, NC and London: Duke University Press, 2020), 313 of 18788, Kindle.

94 Judy, *Sentient Flesh*, 3687 of 18788, Kindle.

wheat. In 1765 at the age of thirty-seven, Venture Smith redeemed his body, purchased his freedom. Smith then went on to redeem his two sons Solomon and Cuff and his pregnant wife Meg, who were held in slavery by Thomas Stanton, and his daughter Hannah, who was enslaved by Ray Mumford.[95]

Redemption materialized as solidarity. Smith redeemed three enslaved Black men unrelated to him by blood, paying sixty pounds, four hundred dollars, and twenty-five pounds, respectively. Venture Smith redeemed these men "for no other reason than to oblige them."[96]

Redemption materialized through disguise, evasion, and escape. Married couple Ellen and William Craft in 1848 disguised themselves to liberate themselves. Dressed in male attire, head and face swaddled in cloth, and complaining of infected teeth and a rheumatic hand, Ellen's fair skin color allowed her to *pass* (pose) as an ailing White male slaveholder traveling with 'his' enslaved valet. Using steamboat and train, the pair successfully made their way from Savannah, Georgia, to Charleston, South Carolina,

---

[95] Venture Smith, "A Narrative of the Life and Adventures of Venture, a Native of Africa: but Resident above Sixty Years in the United States of America. Related by Himself," 1–31, in James Brewer Stewart, ed. *Venture Smith and the Business of Slavery and Freedom* (Amherst and Boston: University of Massachusetts Press, 2010).

[96] Smith, "A Narrative of the Life and Adventures of Venture," 31.

to Philadelphia, Pennsylvania. Warned by a sympathetic lodge keeper that slavecatchers were in the area, the Crafts quickly made their way to Boston and settled down to gain more education and to work—William as a cabinet maker, Ellen as a seamstress. Their plans were frustrated, when slaveholders emboldened by Congressional passage of the Fugitive Slave Act (1850) issued a warrant for their seizure and return. After eluding slavecatchers for three or four days, Ellen and William Craft succeeded in boarding a British ship and reached Liverpool, England three months later.[97]

From about the age of fifteen, Harriet Jacobs (writing as Linda Brent) adamantly resisted the salacious sexual advances of slaveholder and physician James Norcom (aka Dr. Flint). Later, when Norcom threatened to sell her two young children, Jacobs stood her ground. In June 1835, she resolved to run away. For seven years, Jacobs evaded the physician by 'hiding in (near) plain sight' in a cramped attic space—nine feet by seven feet, and about three feet in height—above a shed in her grandmother Molly Horniblow's yard. When Jacobs inspected the constricted space, she found a gimlet (a hand tool for drilling small holes) that her uncle inadvertently left behind when he

---

[97] John W. Blassingame, ed., *Slave Testimony: Two Centuries of Letters, Speeches, Interviews, and Autobiographies* (Baton Rouge and London: Louisiana State University Press, 1977), 268–74.

devised a trap door through which food and other articles might be transferred. Jacobs bored a series of small holes in the wall for air and light, allowing her to breathe more easily, to read, and to catch glimpses of her son and daughter during their visits with her grandmother. In 1842, Harriet Jacobs fled North; Norcom searched for her obsessively, employing slavecatchers to pursue her in Northern cities.[98]

In 1849, to escape enslavement, Henry 'Box' Brown had himself shipped from Virginia to abolitionists in Philadelphia. As a child, his mother instructed him in moral principles, taught him about God, and urged him to pray. Brown came to believe that God would direct his escape from bondage if he prayed sincerely.

> At length after praying earnestly to [God], who seeth afar off, for assistance, in my difficulty, suddenly, as if from above, there darted into my mind these words, "Go and get a box, and put yourself into it." I pondered the words over in my mind. "Get a box,?" thought I; "what can this mean?" But I was "not disobedient unto the heavenly vision," and I determined to put into practice this direction, as I considered it, from my heavenly Father.[99]

---

98 Harriet A. Jacobs, *Incidents in the Life of a Slave Girl* (1861; New York: Harcourt Brace Jovanovich, Publishers, 1973).

99 Henry Brown, *Narrative of the Life of Henry Box Brown* (Boston: Brown & Stearns, 1849), 707 of 1137, Kindle.

With the aid of parishioners of a local church, Henry Brown got into a box that was 3 feet long by 2 feet 8 inches deep by 2 feet wide and was posted to Philadelphia. Reportedly, after twenty-seven hours, he emerged a free man, praising God.[100]

Redemption materialized through codes. Singing Spirituals, enslaved people conveyed coded messages signaling plans for escape and warning of impending danger. Regard such Spirituals as "Steal way" or "Go Down, Moses" or "Swing Low, Sweet Chariot" or "Bound for Canaan Land." Fugitive slave, abolitionist, journalist, and orator Frederick Douglass testified to the power of the Spirituals: "They were tones, loud, long and deep; they breathed the prayer and complaint of soils boiling over with the bitterest anguish. Every tone was a testimony against slavery, and a prayer to God for deliverance from chains."[101]

Redemption materialized in risk. Harriet Tubman symbolized all that liberation, deliverance, and redemption meant to enslaved peoples; she signified

---

100 Brown, *Narrative of the Life of Henry Box Brown*, 744 of 1137, Kindle.

101 Frederick Douglass, *Narrative of the Life of Frederick Douglass: An American Slave Written by Himself* (1845; Cambridge, MA and London: The Belknap Press, 1960), 37; Jean M. Humez, *Harriet Tubman: The Life and the Life Stories* (Madison: The University of Wisconsin Press, 2003), 234–35.

freedom, possibility, and promise. Tubman conducted her family members out of slavery, then risked nineteen trips on the Underground Railroad, redeeming at least seventy people from the Egypt of American slavery. "Walking by night and hiding by day, [using] song codes for secret communication,"[102] Tubman's *self-sacrificing risk* illuminated the social and communal character of redemption and enfleshed the guiding presence and power of the God of the Enslaved. One man whom Tubman led out of enslavement and into Canada told an interviewer that those traveling with her were not afraid of being recaptured. "The Lord has given Moses the power," he declared.[103] Harriet Tubman *was* Moses.

III. Chattel Slavery and Christianity

The enslaved people encountered Christianity under the most stifling and constrictive existential, mental, and physical circumstances—chattel slavery. Chattel slavery in the North American colonies, and then in the United States, functioned on the 'fiction' that Black children, women, and men were not human, but 'chattel,' movable objects or articles of personal property—consumable, fungible, mortgageable, sellable, usable, disposable. Chattel slavery

---

102 Humez, *Harriet Tubman*, 43.

103 Humez, *Harriet Tubman*, 259.

assaulted the enslaved person's humanity through discursive and psychic (de)formation that taught enslaved women and men from childhood to view themselves as property,[104] thus, aiming to alienate the enslaved from all that constitutes human being-in-the-world—history, heritage, memory, family and kin, individuality, idiosyncrasies, anxieties, and desires. Chattel slavery sought to achieve such devastation through physical and psychic violence which sealed enslaved people in a condition of extreme fear, thus, constantly renewing "the shock of slavery,"[105] and, thereby, attempting to stifle every glimmer of a hope of freedom.

In the eighteenth century, the majority of Anglo-American Protestant slaveholders demonstrated considerable reluctance to expose enslaved people to the Bible or to baptize them. These planters were fearful that under then-applicable British law, Christian baptism would compel manumission. Anglican minister Francis Le Jau, preaching in Goose Creek, South Carolina under the auspices of the Society for the Propagation of the Gospel (SPG), made enslaved candidates take the following oath prior to being baptized: "You declare in the presence of God and before this congregation that you do not ask for the holy baptism out of design to

---

104 Johnson, *Soul by Soul*, 20–24.

105 Scott C. Williamson, *The Narrative Life: The Moral and Religious Thought of Frederick Douglass* (Macon, GA: Mercer University Press, 2002), 36.

The Politics of Redemption

free yourself from the duty and obedience you owe to your master while you live, but meekly for the good of your soul."[106]

Despite weak and unenforced objections to racial slavery by the Vatican, Catholic laity, priests, bishops, and religious orders of women and men involved themselves with the creed, custom, commerce, and culture of slaveholding. In the French Catholic colony of Louisiana, the Code Noir of 1724 required slaveholders to instruct the enslaved people in Catholic doctrine. On the one hand, much like their Protestant counterparts, many Catholic planters displayed a lack of interest and care in meeting this obligation. On the other hand, some Catholic and Protestant planters did cooperate with missionaries in the effort at evangelization. In 1785, John Carroll, "superior of the American missions, in his report to Rome on the state of the Church in the United States," numbered the Catholic population in Maryland as 15,800, of whom more than 3,000 were enslaved.[107] By now, it is well-known that in the 1820s the Maryland Province of the Society of

---

106 Martha Washington Creel, *"A Peculiar People:" Slave Religion and the Community Culture among the Gullahs* (New York and London: New York University Press, 1988), 101.

107 Albert Raboteau, *Slave Religion: The 'Invisible Institution' in the Antebellum South* (Oxford: Oxford University Press, 1975), 112–13.

Jesus, the Jesuits, was one of the nation's largest slaveholders. Even during that period, the Jesuits' 1838 sale of 272 enslaved Black Catholics to Louisiana planters in order to meet debts associated with Georgetown University was viewed widely as "scandalous."[108]

Having shut the door of Christian baptism to human beings deemed merchandise or commodities, slaveholders began to reconsider; they maintained that Baptism might render the enslaved people less rebellious and more pliable to accept their fate. So, on some plantations, the enslaved people attended church along with White slaveholders and their families, sitting or standing in designated areas, even "listening to the same sermons, the same songs, and the same prayers."[109] One enslaved woman, Annie

---

108 See Thomas Murphy, *Jesuit Slaveholding in Maryland, 1717–1838* (New York: Routledge, 2001), 100; The Georgetown Slavery Archive, http://slaveryarchive.georgetown.edu, James J. Hennesey, *American Catholics: A History of the Roman Catholic Community* in the *United States* (New York: Oxford University Press, 1981), Cyprian Davis, *The History of Black Catholics in the United States* (New York: Crossroad Publishing, 1990), Patrick W. Carey, *Catholics in America: A History*, rev. ed. (Westport, CT: Praeger Publishers, 2004), Robert Emmett Curran, *Shaping American Catholicism: Maryland and New York, 1805–1915* (Washington, D.C.: Catholic University of American Press, 2012).

109 John B. Cade, "Out of the Mouths of Ex-Slaves," *The Journal of Negro History* 20, no. 3 (July 1935): 327.

Washington, told her interviewer that the Black people "sat on the floor of the church or [outside on] steps and peeped in."[110]

Some planters allowed White clerics to preach to the enslaved people in the slave quarters; these men put Christian theology to dubious purpose. Anglican minister Thomas Bacon published a sermon that exhorted the enslaved people to accept their bondage as part of a natural and divinely ordained social order in which masters were "God's overseers" and slaves were to obey these masters as if they were obeying God.[111] White ministers frequently employed the hermeneutics of sacrifice and servitude in their proslavery arguments. James Furman, a Baptist cleric from South Carolina, declared: "We who own slaves honor God's law in the exercise of our authority."[112]

In *A Brief Examination of Scripture Testimony on the Institution of Slavery*, Minister Thornton Stringfellow of Culpeper County, Virginia, contended that slavery derived from Noah's curse of the progeny of Canaan. He contended that the descendants

---

110 Cade, "Out of the Mouths of Ex-Slaves," 328.

111 Thomas Bacon, "A Sermon to Maryland Slaves" (1749), 77, 83, 86, in *Religion in American History: A Reader*, ed. Jon Butler and Harry Stout (New York: Oxford University Press, 1998).

112 Donald Matthews, *Religion in the Old South* (Chicago: University of Chicago Press, 1977), 136.

of Canaan were to be servants of servants—at the mercy of their kin. In exegeting the text, Stringfellow stated that the language used showed "the *favor* which God would exercise to the posterity of Shem and Japheth, while they were holding the posterity of Ham in a state of *abject bondage*." He continued:

> May it not be said in truth, that God decreed this institution before it existed; and has he not connected its existence, with prophetic tokens of special favor, to those who should be slave owners or masters? He is the same God now that he was when he gave these views of his moral character to the world.[113]

Stringfellow drew a direct line from Noah's curse of the descendants of Ham (Canaan's offspring) to the divinely ordained enslavement of Black people in nineteenth-century America. He concluded: "God decreed slavery—and shows in that decree, tokens of good-will to the master."[114]

---

113 Thornton Stringfellow, *A Brief Examination of Scripture Testimony on the Institution of Slavery, In an Essay, first published in the Religious Herald, and republished by request: with Remarks on a Letter of Elder* Galusha, *of New York, to Dr. R. Fuller, of South Carolina*, 2. Author's italics. http://docsouth.unc.edu/church/stringfellow/stringfellow.html.

114 Stringfellow, *A Brief Examination of Scripture Testimony*, 2. Author's italics.

Bishop Meade advocated a double doctrine of Jesus as the servant-of-servants and applied this to both slaveholders and slaves. According to Meade, Jesus "chose the form of a servant and became the *servant-of-servants*, illustrating [the] blessed doctrine [of slavery] by his own meek, patient, suffering life."[115] Since Jesus was "faultless in word and deed toward those in bondage," slaveholders were to imitate him by correct, perfect 'Christian' behavior toward those whom they held in slavery. And since Jesus had been meek and humble, enslaved women and men were to imitate him by accepting their enslavement meekly and humbly, without protest; their perpetual servitude was ordained by God's divine will.[116]

Frank Roberson, a freed man, paraphrased a typical sermon by White preachers:

> You slaves will go to heaven if you are good, but don't ever think that you will be close to your mistress and master. No! No! there will be a wall between you; but there will be holes in it that will permit you to look out and see your mistress when she passes by. If you want to sit behind this wall, you must do the language of the text 'Obey your masters.'[117]

---

115 Riggins Earl, *Dark Symbols, Obscure Signs: God, Self, and Community in the Slave Mind* (Maryknoll, NY: Orbis Books, 1993), 33.

116 Earl, *Dark Symbols, Obscure Signs*, 33.

117 Cade, "Out of the Mouths of Ex-Slaves," 329.

Lucretia Alexander, Wes Beady, and Richard Carruthers corroborated the regularity of such debased injunctions. Carruthers declared:

> When the white preacher come, he preach and pick up his Bible and claim he getting' the text right out of the good Book and he preach. "The Lord say, don't you [slaves] steal chickens from your missus. Don't you steal your master's hogs." That would be all he preach.[118]

Beady added that no minister said, "nary a word 'bout havin' a soul to save."[119] One slaveholder went so far as to blasphemously pronounce: "I am your only God," and instructed a shameless preacher to proclaim, "Honor your missus and your massa that your days may be long."[120]

In his magisterial study of the Negro Spiritual, John Lovell comments that the enslaved people "retained much of the African's tendency to consider

---

118 Norman R. Yetman, ed., *Voices from Slavery* (New York: Holt, Rinehart and Winston, 1970), 53.

119 George P. Rawick, ed. *The American Slave: A Composite Autobiography* (Westport, CT: Greenwood Publishing Co., 1972), vol. 1 *From Sunup to Sundown: The Making of the Black Community*, 36.

120 George P. Rawick, ed., *The American Slave: A Composite Autobiography* (Westport, CT: Greenwood Publishing Co, 1972), vol. 3, part 4, 192, cited in Henry H. Mitchell, *Black Belief: Folk Beliefs of Blacks in America and West Africa* (New York: Harper & Row Publishers, 1975), 98.

religion as a totality, a unifying element in life," enslaved women and men grasped the dissonance between the actions or behavior of slaveholders and their profession of Christian faith.[121] In her autobiography, *Incidents in the Life of a Slave Girl*, Harriet Jacobs relates a painful incident during a Methodist class meeting.[122] Already heavy-hearted, Jacobs sits beside a grieving enslaved mother. The distressed woman was approached by the class leader, the town constable, whom Jacobs describes as a man who publicly whipped enslaved people, who was a slave trader. "Sister, can you tell us how the Lord deals with your soul?" he asked. "Do you love him as you did formerly?" The woman wept aloud, praying for her children who had been sold from the plantation where she and they had been held. Jacobs continues:

> [The woman] sat down, quivering in every limb. I saw that constable class leader become crimson in the face with suppressed laughter, while he held up his handkerchief, that those who were weeping

---

121 John Lovell, Jr., *Black Song: The Forge and the Flame, The Story of How the Afro-American Spiritual Was Hammered Out* (New York: The Macmillan Company, 1972), 181.

122 Jacobs, *Incidents in the Life of a Slave Girl*, 91. Even in the twenty-first century, the Methodist class meeting continues to be an opportunity for small groups of believers to share their religious experiences and to encourage one another to grow in faith and virtue as disciples of Jesus Christ.

with the poor woman's calamity might not see his merriment. Then, with assumed gravity, he said to the bereaved mother, "Sister, pray to the Lord that every dispensation of his divine will may be sanctified to the good of your poor needy soul."[123]

Such cruelty and hypocrisy underscores what Jacobs identified as the "great difference between Christianity and religion [in] the south." She asserted: "No wonder the slaves sing—'Ole Satan's church is here below / Up to God's free church I hope to go." [124] Joseph Pennington, a fugitive from Maryland slavery and Presbyterian minister, bluntly questioned whether God, although "disapproving of slavery could have brought about good in some other way."[125] Still, in a letter to his parents and siblings, he urged them "not to be prejudiced against the gospel because it may be seemingly twisted into a support of slavery. The gospel rightly understood, taught, received, felt and practised, is anti-slavery as it is anti-sin."[126] The enslaved people recognized the attempts of slaveholders to

---

123 Jacobs, *Incidents in the Life of a Slave Girl*, 91.

124 Jacobs, *Incidents in the Life of a Slave Girl*, 96, 97.

125 James Pennington, *Fugitive Blacksmith, or, Events in the History of James W. C. Pennington, Pastor of a Presbyterian Church, New York, Formerly a Slave in the State of Maryland, United States* 3rd ed. (London: Charles Gilpin Publishers, 1850), 76.

126 Pennington, *The Fugitive Blacksmith*, 76.

anesthetize and to coopt the gospel "as an attractive device for [their] control."[127]

Yet, enslaved people met the alienation and brutality of chattel slavery through creatively transforming their created existence and defending their human dignity and personhood.[128] These religious virtuosos realized themselves through spiritual self-transcendence. Historian Gayraud Wilmore notes that "from the beginning the religion of the descendants of [enslaved] Africans has been something less and something more than what is generally regarded as Christianity."[129] The enslaved people formed a distinctive image of themselves and fashioned "an inner world, a scale of values and fixed points of vantage from which to judge the world around them and themselves."[130] Jewish

---

127 Winthrop D. Jordan, *White over Black: American Attitudes toward the Negro, 1550–1812* (Baltimore: Penguin Books, 1969), 191.

128 See, Beverly Eileen Mitchell, "The African American Struggle for Human Dignity in Chattel Slavery and Afterwards," in *T & T Clark Handbook of African American Theology*, ed., Frederick L. Ware, et al (London: T & T Clark, 2019), 9–18.

129 Gayraud S. Wilmore, *Black Religion and Black Radicalism: An Interpretation of the Religious History of African Americans* 3rd ed (Maryknoll, NY: Orbis Books, 1998), 22.

130 Paul Radin, "Status, Fantasy, and Christian Dogma: Foreword to the First Edition," in *God Struck Me Dead: Voices of Ex-Slaves*, ed. Clifton H. Johnson (1969; Cleveland: Pilgrim Press, 1993), vii.

anthropologist Paul Radin affirms my intuition that enslaved Africans were not "converted" to the putative anti-black God of the slaveholders, but "converted" the God of Jesus to themselves and to their cause of liberation and emancipation.[131] Given the attributes of God as enumerated in classical theism (e.g., immutability, impassibility, omnipotence, omniscience, and omnipresent) such an astonishing claim is not patient of conventional theological or philosophical reasoning. At the same time, the biblical God of Jesus shows the Divineself as love, compassion, mercy, and justice—a God converted by and to the enslaved people.

How did the enslaved people learn about and meet God? By law and custom the enslaved Africans were forbidden to learn to read or to write. Many slaveholders viciously beat enslaved children, youth, and adults whom they found reading or teaching others to read, and some slaveholders severed the forefinger from the right hand of those whom they suspected or caught writing. Initially many slaveholders and clerics refused and were reluctant to extend Christian instruction and sacraments to enslaved people, even weaponized the Gospel of life against them. Lovell contends that the enslaved people learned of God as they "learned about most other things, through [the] grapevine—a few slaves

---

131 Radin, "Status, Fantasy, and Christian Dogma," ix.

listening or observing, a few slaves reading, and the information bursting through the veins and arteries of the slave community like the rush of blood."[132] We might say that their knowledge of the content and message of the Bible, their apprehension of the God of Abraham, Isaac, and Jacob was obtained through gleaning phrases and "eavesdropping," and "overhearing the Gospel."[133]

The enslaved Africans heard and listened to public readings, to prayers held by slaveholding families in their drawing rooms, and to sermons or fragments of sermons. They pondered certain words and phrases, passages and parables; reflected and discussed possible meanings; took up life-giving words and treasured them in their hearts. Over time, portions of biblical books or chapters or passages were memorized and repeated, reshaped and restated. A hermeneutics of suspicion and of recovery were at work in their minds, imaginations, and hearts. Purged of malicious meanings, certain passages and events stood out as pertinent and became the subject of personal

---

132 Lovell, Jr., *Black Song*, 181.

133 Charles H. Long, "Bodies in Time and the Healing of Spaces: Religion, Temporalities, and Health," in *The Collected Writings of Charles H. Long: Ellipsis* (New York: Bloomsbury Publishing, 2018), 273 of 425, Kindle. Long writes that the African American educator Lawrence C. Jones "coined the phrase, 'they overheard the Gospel,' in explaining the reception of Christianity among enslaved people.

and communal meditation and prayer and sermonic re-interpretation. In spite of slavocracy's debasement of Christianity and the ideological distortion of certain verses, the Bible came to occupy a pivotal place in the religio-cultural life of the enslaved peoples. "African Americans," New Testament scholar Allen Callahan tells us, "are the children of slavery in America. And, the Bible, as no other book, is the book of slavery's children."[134] Biblical characters, stories and events, themes and images gave hope to the struggle of Black women and men for freedom, emancipation, redemption, liberation in this world and rejoicing in the next.

Womanist biblical scholar Renita Weems argues that since the enslaved peoples' "earliest exposure to the Bible was aural and set within the context of a slaveholding society,"[135] they were not bound intellectually or morally to any *official* written text, translation, or interpretation, they created for themselves an oral text of the Bible that displayed affinities with the prophetic and apocalyptic traditions

---

134 Allen Dwight Callahan, *The Talking Book: African Americans and the Bible* (New Haven, CT and London: Yale University Press, 2006), xi.

135 Renita J. Weems, "Reading *Her* Way through the Struggle: African American Women and the Bible," in Cain Hope Felder, ed., *Stony the Road We Trod: African American Biblical Interpretation*, Thirtieth Anniversary Expanded Edition, ed., Cain Hope Felder (Minneapolis: Fortress Press, 2021), 77 of 352, Kindle. Author's italics.

of the Hebrew Scriptures. She points out, that since enslaved communities

> were illiterate, they were, therefore, without allegiance to any official text, translation, or interpretation; hence once they heard biblical passages read and interpreted to them, they in turn were free to remember and repeat in accordance with their own interests and tastes. Sermons preached by slave preachers attest amply to the ways in which slaves retold the biblical message in accordance with their own tastes and hermeneutic. Hence, for those raised within an aural culture, retelling the Bible became one hermeneutical strategy, and resistance to the Bible, or portions of it, would become another.[136]

If their initial confrontation with the Bible provoked "suspicion and awe," the enslaved people soon began to associate the Bible with power; indeed, their "capacity and willingness to engage the Bible in a self-interested and, affirming manner" demonstrated their determination to manage life in the strange reality of chattel slavery, to survive, and to achieve freedom.[137]

---

136 Weems, "Reading *Her* Way through Struggle," 75 of 352, Kindle. Author's italics.

137 Vincent Wimbush, "The Bible and African Americans: An Outline of an Interpretative History," in *Stony the Road We Trod*, 100, 101 of 352, Kindle.

Freedom was the dominant theme and object of the religion of the enslaved peoples. Desire and struggle for freedom did not splinter into the dichotomous or oppositional. Rather, the freedom for which they longed, struggled, fought, and died was simultaneously social *and* religious, psychological *and* spiritual, metaphysical *and* ontological, this-worldly *and* other-worldly. Despite the efforts of slaveholders and the institution that sustained them, Jesus came to mean freedom. As theologian Howard Thurman observes, "It was dangerous to let the slave understand that the life and teachings of Jesus meant freedom for the captive and release for those held in economic, social, and political bondage."[138] To understand the fearless and dangerous Jesus was to break the spell cast by the prevailing dominative consciousness, to break with a servile mentality. To understand the fearless and dangerous Jesus was to redeem the Word of God from the grip of slaveholders and set it working free in the midst of those yearning to be free. Jesus meant freedom; Jesus *was* freedom.

Freedom may have been precarious, elusive, and unpredictable, but the struggle for its actual or material realization was rooted in the spirit of the enslaved people. One freed man recalled, "I've heard [the slaves] pray for freedom. I thought it was foolishness, then, but the old-time folks always felt they

---

138 Howard Thurman, *Deep River and The Negro Spiritual Speaks of Life and Death* (Indiana: Friends Untied Press, 1975), 16.

was to be free. It must have been something [re]vealed unto 'em."[139] The enslaved people empowered themselves for redemption, for liberation through their hearing and retelling of the exodus story. They not only interpreted their experience in light of the Bible but interpreted the Bible in light of their experience. They formulated a normative claim for biblical interpretation in the Black community: the Mighty One who liberated the Hebrew people is the very God who is the Liberator and Redeemer of Black people, of all who are poor and oppressed:

> Didn't my Lord deliver Daniel
> Deliver Daniel, deliver Daniel
> Deliver Daniel, deliver Daniel
> An' why not-a every man.

Sallie Paul told her interviewer, "God set de slaves free. De Lord do it. It jus like dis, I believes it was intended from God for de slaves to be free an Abraham Lincoln was just de one what present de speech. It was revealed to him en God was de one dat stepped in en fight de battle."[140] Alice Sewell testified to the power of the enslaved people's prayer for freedom and redemption: "God planned dem

---

139 James Mellon, ed., *Bullwhip Days: The Slaves Remember, An Oral History* (New York: Avon Books, 1988), 190.

140 Rawick, ed., *The American Slave: A Composite Autobiography*, vol. 7, part 2, 121, cited in Henry Mitchell, *Black Belief*, 109–110.

slave prayers to free us like he did de Israelites, and [the prayers] did."[141] She recalled to her interviewer that enslaved people in the area where she was held

> prayed for freedom. We come four and five miles to pray together to God dat if we don't live to see it, to please let our chillen live to see a better day and be free, so dat dey can give honest and fair service to de Lord and all mankind everywhere.[142]

And Mary Reynolds mused: "I 'members 'bout the days of slavery and I don't 'lieve they ever gwine have slaves no more on this earth. I thank Gawd done took that burden offen his black chillum and I'm aimin' to praise him for it to his face."[143]

IV. The Matter or Material of Redemption

For the enslaved people redemption and deliverance, liberation and freedom were experiential, tactile, palpable, substantial, tangible—*material*. When theologian Olin Moyd asserts that "redemption is the root and core motif in Black theology,"[144] not only does he point us to objective and subjective dimensions of redemption, but he also moves us beyond metaphor to the actual objectified bodyperson living

---

141 Yetman, ed., *Voices from Slavery*, 264.

142 Yetman, ed., *Voices from Slavery*, 263.

143 Mellon, ed., *Bullwhip Days*, 23.

144 Moyd, *Redemption in Black Theology*, 7.

within the moldering core of chattel slavery—the living, breathing, moving, acting, loving Blackhuman *bodyperson* is the matter or material of redemption.

Given their collective or communal unyielding and enduring commitment to physical and mental, sexual and gender, cultural and spiritual freedom, enslaved people endeavored *literally* and *actually* to redeem black bodies, their own and the bodies of others. These Blackhuman persons expressed self-transcending love through escaping / shipping / disguising black bodies; through raising / earning / begging / borrowing money to redeem, to buy back, to deliver, to liberate, to ransom, to rescue, to save, to snatch black bodies, their own and others from chattel slavery. In this frightful context and in its haunting afterlife that impinges upon and irrupts into our contemporary, redemption was not, is not, and can never be merely metaphor. In this context, the notion of redemption generates concrete expectations of deliverance and liberation, recovery and retrieval, salvation and achievement.

Like the enslaved Hebrews of the Bible, enslaved Black people did not spiritualize redemption; rather, redemption was about the material, about flesh, about the body and bodily integrity, about reclaiming and engaging in relationships. For enslaved Black people, redemption would realize living— lyrical, liberatory, improvisational living; fresh, vibrant, ordinary living; tense and surprising, boring and beautiful living. Redemption would redress bodily theft and abuse, alienation and social death. Redemption would be pharmacopetic;[145] it would heal the psychic, cultural, physical, gender / sexual, social (i.e., political and economic), and legal effects and conditions that negated Blackhuman persons. Those effects and conditions were not *immaterial*. Blackhuman life mattered and matters. The very flesh and blood, hearts and minds, sex and sexuality—the very life and bodypersons of enslaved Blackhuman beings living free constituted the matter, the material for redemption.

From the perspective of the enslaved Black people, God had intervened actively in history on their behalf, even used war to free them and their descendants from chattel slavery. Moreover, God was concerned not only for the redemption of their souls, but the redemption of their bodies. Yet, perhaps, awash in the throes of jubilation, the newly freed Black people had no hint or expectation that God's decree of redemption would be upended or, at least, would not be upended so quickly. Perhaps, initially, these exuberant free Black people had little or no suspicion that the realization of their dream of social, legal, religious, cultural, and personal freedom would be deferred, rendered elusive; that their struggle would continue.

---

145 Theophus H. Smith, *Conjuring Culture: Biblical Formations of Black America* (New York: Oxford University Press, 1994), 216.

V. Turning Black Redemption Upside Down

After nearly two hundred and fifty years of enslavement, in 1865 approximately four million formerly enslaved Black children, youth, women, and men embarked on the psychic, cultural, social (i.e., political and economic), legal, and personal transition from perpetual racialized hereditary bondage to freedom. An extensive federal program of Reconstruction promised Black *material redemption*—citizenship and political participation, schools and education, rights to work for wages and to purchase land, unencumbered religious expression, family stability, psychic comfort, personal and communal development. Freedwomen and -men hoped, hoped actively and creatively, and their hope became "a pillar of cloud by day and a pillar of fire by night" (Exodus 13: 21).

W. E. B. Du Bois argues that Reconstruction also signaled "the attempt [through Black folk] to reconstruct the basis of American democracy from 1860–1880."[146] This was a fraught undertaking not only in the South, but also in the North. The Civil War had been traumatic: more than 620,000 soldiers were killed in battle, and thousands more wounded

---

146 W. E. B. Du Bois, *Black Reconstruction in America: Toward a History of the Part which Black Folk Played in the Attempt to Reconstruct Democracy in America, 1860-1880* (1935; New York: Routledge, 2017), xxv.

and horrifically maimed. Since the war was fought in the South, the land was devasted—fields lay fallow, crops shriveled, trees withered, public roads were in disrepair, barns and storehouses were dilapidated, houses were burned or destroyed or standing abandoned. The economic status of the Southern slaveholding class had been upended, and Northern capitalists recognized opportunities for substantial dividends on investments and easy wealth.

"The year 1871," writes Vann Newkirk, "was a crucible."[147] By that year, Congress had readmitted the secessionist states to the Union,[148] introduced and secured ratification of the Thirteenth, Fourteenth, and Fifteenth Amendments to the

---

147 Vann R. Newkirk II, "How the Negro Spiritual Changed American Popular Music—and America Itself," *The Atlantic* (December 2023) https://www.theatlantic.com/magazine/archive/2023/12/fisk-university-jubilee-singers-choir-history/675813/

148 The states of Alabama, Arkansas, Florida, Georgia, Louisiana, Mississippi North Carolina, South Carolina, Tennessee, Texas, and Virginia comprised the Confederacy. Maryland, Delaware, West Virginia, Kentucky and Missouri were called Border States; these states accepted and practiced slavery but did not join the confederacy. In order to be readmitted to the Union, former slaveholding states were required to make changes in their constitutions that guaranteed that Black people be accorded the legal status of freedom, be recognized as citizens, and Black men be accorded the vote; required to elect new officials under the new constitutional guidelines; and ratify the Fourteenth Amendment.

Constitution of the United States. These Amendments abolished racialized chattel slavery, redefined citizenship, and provided the first federal civil rights law. Black men and women began to enflesh their redemption: the votes of Black men propelled five Black representatives to seats in Congress, the Freedmen's Bureau sent roughly 900 administrative officials throughout the South to advise and assist freedwomen and -men with necessary practicalities such as schools and land purchases. The Department of Justice, also established in 1871, was directed to suppress the Ku Klux Klan which had been founded six years earlier in 1865.

Reconstruction gave freedwomen and -men courage to experiment, to undertake new projects. "Freedmen's towns" or "freedom towns," or "all-Black" towns sprang up across the South, including Africatown (1866) in Alabama, Eatonville (1877) in Florida, Nicodemus (1877) in Kansas, and Mound Bayou (1877) in Mississippi. Considering such towns from a "black utopian perspective," Aaron Robertson "places the seemingly provisional, expedient, and rudimentary at the center of a vision to create a better world."[149] Freedwomen and -men reconstructed their families; many changed the

---

149 Aaron Robertson, *The Black Utopians: Searching for Paradise and the Promise Land in America* (New York: Farrar, Straus & Giroux, 2024), 29 of 385, Kindle.

surnames or first names that had been given to them by slaveholders. "Renaming was often an act of both radical purpose and plain descriptiveness: Freeman remains a common last name today."[150]

From roughly the mid to late 1870s and 1880s, the Supreme Court "issued a series of decisions that rendered the Reconstruction amendments nearly unenforceable; and mass-scale violence and political terrorism paved the way for the restoration of white supremacy in the South."[151] White supremacists hijacked the term redemption "to lend religious as well as political legitimacy to their violent opposition to freedpeople's quest for full citizenship."[152] They claimed that "to reconstruct the South was to redeem the nation,"[153] but the supremacist version of 'reconstruction' or 'redemption' had little to do with the stated intentions of

---

150 Newkirk, "How the Negro Spiritual Changed American Popular Music—and America Itself," *The Atlantic* (December 2023) https://www.theatlantic.com/magazine/archive/2023/12/fisk-university-jubilee-singers-choir-history/675813/

151 Jill Ogline Titus, "Reconstruction," *George Wright Society Parks Stewardship Forum* 36, no. 3 (September 2020), 451–57.

152 Carole Emberton, *Beyond Redemption: Race, Violence and the American South after the Civil War* (Chicago and London: University of Chicago Press, 2013), 13 of 286, Kindle.

153 Emberton, *Beyond Redemption*, 14 of 286, Kindle.

Congress.[154] A few months after the abolition of slavery, former Confederate officers, soldiers, and sympathizers in Tennessee formed the Ku Klux Klan, with former Confederate General Nathan Bedford Forrest as its first "Grand Dragon." The Klan spread to Alabama, Texas, Arkansas, North Carolina, South Carolina, and Louisiana. These supremacists vowed to take back the South, to reassert White people's political and economic control and cultural domination. They used fraud and cheating, manipulation and intimidation, whippings and sexual assault against women, shootings and riots, mutilations and "Negro hunts," murders and lynchings.[155]

In June 1893, three decades after the Emancipation Proclamation and the conclusion of the Civil War, Black Baptist minister S. A. Moseley warned several hundred Black Baptists, mainly sharecroppers and tenant farmers, about the intensifying threats to their rights as citizens, their dignity as Blackhuman persons, their lives and well-being and that of their families. Moseley recounted the story of exodus as *their very own story*: "Since slavery

---

154 Historian Orville Burton states: "Redemption is a beautiful term of religious faith that would be a better label for the promising years from the early 1860s through the early 1870s than so grossly to misconstrue the decades that follow," *The Age of Lincoln* (New York: Hill & Wang, 2007), 299.

155 Du Bois, *Black Reconstruction in America*, 430, 603–33.

[m]any have been our trials, great our conflicts, and bitter our experiences; but out of them the Lord has brought us safe. . . ."[156] Yet their passage into freedom now was being interrupted and imperiled by White mob violence that left in its wake Black "broken-hearted widows, fatherless children, heart sickening friends and relatives, and discouraged citizens who have lost all hope for protection, even for life."[157] Moseley declared: "We have left the borders of Egypt and are now between the [Red] Sea and the Jordan . . . [and] the Walls of Jericho will be made to bow before us. We are only to be strong and courageous, and the victory is sure."[158]

Moseley urged the freedpeople to dig deep into their religious and spiritual reservoir, to stand and fight against the "racist dreams" of those White Southerners who aimed to 'redeem' their homeland from the "Union victory and the political empowerment of former slaves and their descendants."[159] White Southern 'redeemers' had

---

156 E. C. Morris, *Sermons, Addresses, and Reminiscences and Important Correspondence, With a Picture Gallery of Eminent Ministers and Scholars* (Nashville: National Baptist Publishing Board, 1901), 194, 294, cited in John M. Giggie, *After Redemption: Jim Crow and the Transformation of African American Religion in the Delta, 1875–1915* (Oxford: Oxford University Press, 2008), xvi.

157 Giggie, *After Redemption*, xvi.

158 Giggie, *After Redemption*, xvi.

159 Giggie, *After Redemption*, xvi.

> stealthily and ruthlessly stripped [Black people] of the franchise, the right of due process, the chance to attend adequately funded public schools, the ability to travel freely, and most basically, the daily hope of living without the threat of being scorned, mocked, raped, beaten or killed because of the color of their skin.[160]

Former Confederate officers, prominent White male state and local officials blamed Reconstruction and emancipation "for the suffering poor whites experienced. [And thus] pitted poor whites against blacks . . . heightened racial tensions and led the two groups to ignore their common class interests."[161] Further, Southern states enacted 'Black Codes,' laws and ordinances that not only reinscribed and reinforced racial and social hierarchies, but surveilled black bodies and behavior:

> vagrancy laws imposed heavy penalties that reduced black labor to sharecropping and returned black workers to plantations. . . . The laws criminalized 'seditious speech' and 'insulting gestures' (which might mean anything, such as looking whites in the eye, forgetting to remove one's hat in the presence of a white man, failing to tip one's hat in the presence of a white woman, or failing to open a door for whites). Each provision reinforced

---

160 Giggie, *After Redemption*, xvi.
161 Marbury, *Pillars of Cloud and Fire*, 83.

the social hierarchy of the Old South. Finally, these codes made firearms possession illegal to ensure that blacks remained defenseless as the old regime resurged.[162]

The collapse of Reconstruction left Black people groping for answers about the meaning of freedom and redemption. White Southern politicians, landowners, farmers, merchants, and everyday citizens turned Black redemption upside down. Once again, "white supremacy" became the "cornerstone"[163] of political strategies in the Southern states. White racist violence tormented Black people at nearly every turn with intimidation, debt peonage, sexual molestation, lynching or the threat of lynching. Once again, in their very flesh and blood, sex and sexuality, Blackhuman persons were psychically and physically menaced.

---

162 Marbury, *Pillars of Cloud and Fire*, 82.
163 On March 21, 1861, Alexander H. Stephens, the President of the Confederate States of America, gave an extemporaneous address at the Athenaeum in Savannah, Georgia, setting out the thinking of the South on secession: "Our new government's foundations are laid, its corner-stone rests, upon the great truth that the negro is not equal to the white man; that slavery subordination to the superior race is his natural and normal condition. This, our new government, is the first, in the history of the world, based upon this great physical, philosophical, and moral truth," American Battlefield Trust, https://www.battlefields.org/learn/primary-sources/cornerstone-speech.

Dispirited, but not without hope, many Black people set out for a better place—the north. Youth, women, men, entire families formed the 'Great Migration' of the early twentieth century: "the largest resettlement of people of African descent since the close of the slave trade, involving nearly five hundred thousand black Southerners who trekked north from 1915 to 1920 and over one million during the next decade."[164] Yet, the equivocating, evasive legal and political policies written into the United States Constitution permitted segregation, discrimination, intimidation, White mob violence, assault, and lynching to track them north.

VI. Ideals and Laws Supplanted through Duplicity

How did it happen that a serious and daring group of men, inspired by Western European Enlightenment ideals, overthrew a colonizing eighteenth-century superpower to gain political and economic, societal and cultural, religious and moral, personal and collective freedom? How did it happen that that same group of men, who dedicated their lives and sacred honor to uphold and defend divinely given inalienable rights of life, liberty, and pursuit

---

164 Giggie, *After Redemption*, 196; see also, Isabel Wilkerson, *The Warmth of Other Suns: The Epic Story of America's Great Migration* (New York: Random House, 2010).

of happiness, formed a nation and a government that acceded to the practice of chattel slavery? How could these men pass on to their political descendants Enlightenment aims and values, while subjugating and oppressing, legislating and legalizing, enshrining and perpetuating the *unfreedom* of African children, women, and men? How did a nation so conceived within publicly declared values of equality, liberty, and justice consent to exist as a slave society? It was political and economic sleight of hand of the worst sort.

Perhaps, it may be shocking to fully comprehend that the volitional consent of the founders and framers to build a slave society coincided not only with *their* very own revolution for freedom from oppression, but also with the French and Haitian revolutions. Charles Long reminds us that while the Haitian revolution toppled the slave system, the American revolution legitimated and preserved it. "For the American republic this meant that the major societal and cultural institutions that developed from its founding obscured the fact of slavery the same moment that it legitimated the system of slavery."[165] Ira Berlin draws out for us the totalizing impact of chattel slavery in the American republic.

---

165 Long, "Bodies in Time and the Healing of Spaces, Religion, Temporalities, and Health," 264 of 425, Kindle.

> What distinguished societies with slaves was the fact that slaves were marginal to the central productive processes; slavery was just one form of labor among many. . . . In societies with slaves, no one presumed the master-slave relationship to be the social exemplar. . . . In slave societies, by contrast, slavery stood at the center of the economic production, and the master-slave relationship provided the model for all social relations: husband and wife, parent and child, employer and employee, teacher and student. From the most intimate connections between men and women to the most public ones between ruler and ruled, all relationships mimicked those of slavery. As Frank Tannenbaum said, "Nothing escaped, nothing, and no one."[166]

In other words, slavery affected nearly every facet of American life—political and economic, societal and cultural, religious and moral, personal and collective.

Neither the founding documents nor the original Constitution of the United States explicitly mention the words 'slave' or 'slavery.' But, according to Robin Einhorn, "the issue of slavery was debated in the Constitutional Convention on an almost daily basis since this 'peculiar property' was part and parcel of

---

166 Ira Berlin, *Many Thousands Gone* (Cambridge, MA: Harvard University Press, 1998), 8; see Frank Tannenbaum, *Slave and Citizen* (Alfred A. Knopf, 1946; repr. Beacon Press, 1992), 117.

the debates that had to do with taxation, representation, states' rights."[167]

> Consider *Article I, Section 2*, the United States Constitution (1787): Representatives and direct taxes shall be apportioned among the several States which may be included within this union, according to their respective numbers, which shall be determined by adding to the whole number of free persons, including those bound to service for a term of years, and excluding Indians not taxed, three fifths of all other persons.

Section 2 provides for the allocation of Congressional representation (and taxes) on the basis of "the whole number of free persons" and "three fifths of all other persons." Those "other persons" were the enslaved, but they were accorded neither vote nor voice, neither legal rights nor legal standing in the political configuration of the states and the nation. By counting enslaved persons as three-fifths, Southern states created conditions not only for the possibility of an increase in the number of representatives from the Southern states, but also for outsized, domineering national influence. Paul Finkelman notes, "If only free persons were counted,

---

167 Long, "Bodies in Time and the Healing of Spaces, Religion, Temporalities, and Health," 264 of 425, Kindle; see, Robin L. Einhorn, *American Taxation, American Slavery* (Chicago: University of Chicago Press, 2006), 120–124.

The Politics of Redemption

then the Northern states would have dominated Congress. . . . This provision was about the distribution of political power among the states."[168] The Three-Fifths clause armed Southern representatives with "the political muscle" to block federal legislation that opposed slavery and allowed them to "protect the master class of the South."[169]

Robin Einhorn explains that the Three-Fifths clause also obscured tax policies that favored slaveholders. In *A Disquisition on Government*, Senator and later Vice-President John C. Calhoun cast slaveholders as a minority whose rights must be defended and who needed "the power of preventing or arresting the action of government."[170]

---

168 Paul Finkelman writes: "Despite popular understandings, this provision did not declare that African Americans were three-fifths of a person. Rather, the provision declared that the slave states would get extra representation in Congress for their slaves, even though those states treated slaves purely as property," "The Three-Fifths Clause: Why Its Taint Persists," *The Root* (February 2, 2013), https://www.theroot.com/three-fifths-clause-why-its-taint-persists-1790895387.

169 Finkelman, "The Three-Fifths Clause: Why Its Taint Persists," https://www.theroot.com/three-fifths-clause-why-its-taint-persists-1790895387.

170 John C. Calhoun, *A Disquisition on Government and a Discourse on the Constitution and Government of the United States* (1851; New York: D. Appleton and Co., 1853), cited in Einhorn, *American Taxation, American Slavery*, 249.

Calhoun aimed to shield slaveholders from government encroachment on their property rights, that is, their rights to own and to dispose of human beings. The spread and consolidation of Enlightenment ideals such as liberty, fraternity, equality, tolerance, and progress made slavery "inherently vulnerable."[171] To take these ideals with full political seriousness exposes the duplicity of both Southern arguments that would "guarantee the power of the slaveholders—over their slaves but also over everyone else"[172] and Northern arguments that simultaneously criticized and tolerated slavery, while restricting participation in government exclusively to *free White men*. Einhorn points out that "Slaveholders would not permit majorities, even of southern white men, to make decisions affecting their 'property.' Slaveholders would not allow nonslaveholders to decide how to tax."[173]

---

171 Einhorn, *American Taxation, American Slavery*, 250.

172 Einhorn, *American Taxation, American Slavery*, 253.

173 Einhorn, *American Taxation, American Slavery*, 250. Einhorn brings this argument into our writhing contemporary: "The antigovernment rhetoric that continues to saturate our political life is rooted in slavery rather than liberty. The American mistrust of government is not part of our democratic heritage. It comes from slaveholding elites who had no experience with democratic governments where they lived and knew only one thing about democracy: that it threatened slavery. The idea that government is the primary danger to liberty has

In a few states free Black men could vote, Black women could not vote, and White women had very limited access to the franchise.[174] Feminist historian Jan Lewis traces the failure to explicitly mention women in the Constitution. James Wilson, a delegate from Pennsylvania, proposed that representation in the lower house should be "in proportion to the whole number of white & other free citizens & inhabitants of every age sex & condition including those bound to servitude for a term of years and

---

many sources, but one of its main sources in the United States involved the "liberty" of some people to hold other people as chattel property," *American Taxation, American Slavery*, 7–8.

174 The original Constitution left the assignment of voting rights and regulations to the states. In the early days of the Republic, free Black men could vote but soon lost the right to vote in the states of New Jersey, Maryland, and Connecticut, although this seems not to be the case in Pennsylvania. In 1807, New Jersey's state legislature amended their constitution to restrict the vote to tax-paying White male citizens. The first place in the United States to enfranchise women after New Jersey was the Wyoming Territory, which passed women's suffrage on December 10, 1869. Every state that joined the Union after 1819 explicitly limited voting rights to White men. In 1855, only Maine, Massachusetts, New Hampshire, Rhode Island, and Vermont permitted Black male voters https://www.yourvoteyourvoicemn.org/past/communities/african-americans-past/african-american-voting-rights-civil-war/right-vote-expands.

three-fifths of all other persons not comprehended in the foregoing description, except Indians not paying taxes, in each state."[175] The delegates "accepted Wilson's language," but the editing committee returned wording that today we recognize as Article I, Section 2.[176] Lewis comments:

> The term "women" ended up on the cutting room floor, but we can, and should, understand that women were indeed included in the term "free persons," and, hence, that every place that the Constitution uses the term "person" or "persons" and probably every other place that it uses gender- neutral language as well, women were implicitly included.[177]

Lewis concludes her analysis noting that "the Constitution made women rights-bearing citizens and

---

175 *The Records of the Federal Convention of 1787*, ed. Max Farrand (1911; repr., 4 volumes, New Haven, CT, 1966), I, 202, cited in Jan Lewis, "Representation of Women in the Constitution," 24, in *Women and the U. S. Constitution: History, Interpretation, and Practice*, eds., Sibyl A. Schwarzenbach and Patricia Smith (New York: Columbia University Press, 2003), 24.

176 Lewis, "Representation of Women in the Constitution," 24. Four states—New Jersey, Wyoming, Utah, and Colorado—can claim for various reasons to be the first state to grant women's suffrage, https://www.historycolorado.org/story/womens-history/2019/07/25/which-state-had-womens-suffrage-first

177 Lewis, "Representation of Women in the Constitution," 24.

represented them as members of the body politic, but it gave them no means of securing their rights."[178] Yet, the term 'women' denoted White women exclusively. The Constitution left the assignment of voting rights to the states. And, for a short time, New Jersey allowed women to vote, but by 1807 amended their constitution to restrict voting to tax-paying White male citizens. Wyoming passed women's suffrage in 1869.

> *Article I, Section 9*, the United States Constitution (1787): The migration and importation of such persons as any of the states now existing shall think proper to admit, shall not be prohibited by the Congress prior to the year one thousand eight hundred and eight, but a tax or duty may be imposed on such importation, not exceeding ten dollars for each person.

Section 9 forbids Congressional interference with the (unnamed, but implied) trade in black bodies for two decades after ratification of the Constitution. This provision, notes distinguished jurist A. Leon Higginbotham, "assure[d] each state the option of perpetuating slavery."[179] This was another

---

178 Lewis, "Representation of Women in the Constitution," 30.
179 Higginbotham, *Shades of Freedom: Racial Politics and Presumptions of the American Legal Process* (New York: Oxford University Press, 1996), 69.

constitutionally approved victory for the Southern states and their commitment to slavery.

> *Article IV, Section 2*, the United States Constitution (1787): No person held to service or labor in one state, under the laws thereof, escaping into another, shall, in consequence of any law or regulation therein, be discharged from such service or labor, but shall be delivered up on claim of the party to whom such service or labor may be due.

Again, without using the words 'slavery' or 'slave,' this clause insinuates the existence of slavery and enslaved persons in the United States. The enslaved person belongs to or is owned by the slaveholder (master) and cannot be relieved of her or his service or labor without the master's consent. With passage of the Fugitive Slave Act (1793 and 1850), Congress reinforced this Article, thus prohibiting enslaved persons from jury trials and from testifying on their own behalf. Federal marshals who refused to enforce this law and individuals who aided fugitives were penalized severely.

Issued on the first day of January 1863, the Emancipation Proclamation was limited in scope: it did not release all enslaved Black persons from chattel slavery, but only those held in bondage in seceding states. Black persons enslaved in Union and in non-rebellious Southern states remained in bondage literally and legally under state laws. Moreover, slavery was not abolished in the rebellious states.

> Consider the *Thirteenth Amendment* to the U. S. Constitution (1865): *Section 1*: Neither slavery nor involuntary servitude, except as a punishment for crime whereof the party shall have been duly convicted, shall exist within the United States, or any place subject to their jurisdiction.
>
> *Section 2*: Congress shall have the power to enforce this article by appropriate legislation.

For more than seventy-five years, beginning with the Continental Congress, successive legislators, judges, and presidents obscured the existence of slavery or slaves in the nation's founding document. Yet slavery was crucial to the wealth of the colonies that resisted taxation without British parliamentary representation. "It is indeed ironic," Higginbotham observes, "that the first time the word 'slavery' appeared in the United States Constitution was when the institution of slavery was abolished by ratification of the Thirteenth Amendment in December 1865."[180]

---

180 Higginbotham, *Shades of Freedom*, 68. Delaware ratified the Thirteenth Amendment in 1901, Kentucky ratified the Amendment in 1976, and Mississippi did so in 1995, formally filing the ratification paperwork in 2013, see *Reconstruction in America: Racial Violence after the Civil War, 1865–1876* (Montgomery, AL: Equal Justice Initiative, 2020), 107 n34, n35, n36.

Consider the *Fourteenth Amendment* to the U. S. Constitution (1868) *Section 1*: All persons born or naturalized in the United States, and subject to the jurisdiction thereof, are citizens of the United States and of the State wherein they reside. No State shall make or enforce any law which shall abridge the privileges or immunities of citizens of the United States; nor shall any State deprive any person of life, liberty, or property, without due process of law; nor deny to any person within its jurisdiction the equal protection of the laws.

Section 2: Representatives shall be apportioned among the several States according to their respective numbers, counting the whole number of persons in each State, excluding Indians not taxed. But when the right to vote at any election for the choice of electors for President and Vice-President of the United States, Representatives in Congress, the Executive and Judicial officers of a State, or the members of the Legislature thereof, is denied to any of the male inhabitants of such State, being twenty-one years of age, and citizens of the United States, or in any way abridged, except for participation in rebellion, or other crime, the basis of representation therein shall be reduced in the proportion which the number of such male citizens shall bear to the whole number of male citizens twenty-one years of age in such State.

The framers of the Constitution seem to have simply assumed that there is citizenship of the United

States and of the States; thus, they provided no explicit rule about this. In order to 'define' the status of freed Black people, the Fourteenth Amendment also defined the citizenship of the nation.

During the senatorial debate on the Fourteenth Amendment, Maine Senator Lot M. Morrill of Maine grasped the importance of its passage:

> If there is anything with which the American people are troubled, and if there is anything with which the American statesman is perplexed and vexed, it is what to do with the negro, how to define him, what he is in American Law, and what rights he is entitled to. What shall we do with the everlasting, inevitable negro? is the question which puzzles all brains and vexes all statesmen. Now, as a definition, this amendment [to Section I which establishes the citizenship of the native of African descent] settles it. Hitherto we have said that he was nondescript in our statutes; he had no status; he was ubiquitous; he was both man and thing; he was three fifths of a person for representation and he was a thing for commerce and for use. In the highest sense, then . . . this bill is important as a definition.[181]

---

181 Cited in Bill Lawson, "Citizenship and Slavery," in Howard McGary and Bill E. Lawson, *Between Slavery and Freedom: Philosophy and American Slavery* (Bloomington and Indianapolis: Indiana University Press, 1992); 55–56, see also, Cathleen D. Cahill, "Our Democracy and the American Indian: Citizenship, Sovereignty, and the Native Vote in the 1920s," *Journal of Women's History* 32, no. 1 (Spring 2020): 44–51.

The Fourteenth Amendment, ratified on July 8, 1868, granted citizenship to freed Black people and their descendants; but the Amendment did not conclusively settle Black people's civil and political status, nor did it further their full acceptance as human beings by their fellow citizens.[182]

Twenty-two years after the Emancipation Proclamation, Supreme Court Justice Joseph P. Bradley argued against the Civil Right Act of 1875, which provided for equality of access to public accommodations. According to Bradley, the United States government did not have the "authority to prohibit private acts of discrimination; that was the role of the individual states."[183] Two decades later, the Supreme Court declared in Plessy v. Ferguson

---

[182] Thomas Jefferson believed "the two races, equally free, cannot live in the same government. Nature, habit, opinion have drawn indelible lines of distinction between them," Thomas Jefferson, *The Autobiography of Thomas Jefferson* (New York, 1959), 62, cited in John Chester Miller, *The Wolf by the Ears: Thomas Jefferson and Slavery* (New York: The New American Library, 1977), 278. There always were some, even abolitionists, who believed that Black people *did not belong* in the United States or that Black people *could not become full citizens*. Given the scope, intensity, and ubiquity of every-day racism, even some African Americans viewed (and still view) the notion of belonging and the prospect of the free exercise of full citizenship with deep skepticism.

[183] Lawson, "Moral Discourse and Slavery," in *Between Slavery and Freedom*, 71.

(1896) that separate-but-equal facilities were constitutional. The Fourteenth Amendment applied only to political rights (e.g., voting and jury service), not 'social rights' (e.g., seating in public transportation). The Court denied that segregated railroad cars were necessarily inferior. Justice Henry Brown wrote:

> We consider the underlying fallacy of [Plessy's] argument to consist in the assumption that the enforced separation of the two races stamps the colored race with a badge of inferiority. If this be so, it is not by reason of anything found in the act, but solely because the colored race chooses to put that construction upon it.[184]

Justice Brown's decision echoed that delivered by an earlier Court in Dred Scott v. John F. A. Sanford (1857). Here is Roman Catholic Chief Justice Roger Taney writing for the majority (7–2):

> [Black people] had for more than a century before been regarded as beings of an inferior order, and altogether unfit to associate with the white race, either in social or political relations; and so far inferior, that they had no rights which the white man was bound to respect; and that the negro might justly and lawfully be reduced to slavery for

---

184 "Summary of *Plessy v. Ferguson*," http://argumentcentered education.com/wp-content/uploads/2019/08/PlessyvFergusonSummary18.08.01.pdf.

> his benefit. He was bought and sold, and treated as an ordinary article of merchandise and traffic. . . . This opinion was at that time fixed and universal in the civilized portion of the white race. It was regarded as an axiom in morals as well as in politics, which no one thought of disputing or supposed to be open to dispute. . . .[185]

Three decades separate the sermonic address of the Reverend Moseley from the legal opinion of Chief Justice Taney. More than two hundred years earlier in 1664 the legislature of colonial Maryland structured indenture into perpetual and hereditary chattel slavery for Black people. This structuring racialized Blackhuman beings as slaves; slavery 'created' blackness. Thus all (or nearly all) Blackhuman beings were deemed to be slaves (or enslavable). Moreover, since slaves were / are of an inferior order, and Blackhuman beings were / are slaves (or enslavable), Blackhuman beings were / are deemed to be of an inferior order.

Neither Emancipation nor war, neither Reconstruction nor Constitutional Amendment, neither law nor precept—not even abolition would redeem the nation's identification of black skin with slavery, enslavement, enslavableness; with inferiority, deficiency, and powerlessness. Even in our contemporary politics and law mock the very personhood of

---

185 Cited in Higginbotham, *Shades of Freedom*, 65.

Black people, mock redemption, mock justice. Thus, wrote Langston Hughes:

> That Justice is a blind goddess
> Is a thing to which we black are wise:
> Her bandage hides two festering sores
> That once perhaps were eyes.[186]

Political policies and law failed to 'redeem' the stolen lives and dignity of enslaved Black people, failed to protect their bodypersons; failed to incorporate Black children, youth, women, and men into the social contract of the nation. Political policies and law have left the *entire people* of the nation stranded in a "moral / political vocabulary" that remains, even in the twenty-first century, not merely "morally unsatisfactory and inadequate,"[187] but unprincipled, duplicitous, and treacherous. To paraphrase literary theorist Saidiya Hartman: We the people—we the *entire people* of the nation—live in the time of slavery, live in the present that chattel slavery created. This is the ongoing crisis of our American citizenship.[188]

---

186 Langston Hughes, *The Collected Poems of Langston Hughes*, ed. Arnold Rampersad and David Roessel (New York: Random House, 1995), 31.

187 Lawson, "Moral Discourse and Slavery," in *Between Slavery and Freedom*, 72.

188 Saidiya Hartman, *Lose Your Mother: A Journey along the Atlantic Slave Route* (New York: Farrar, Straus and Giroux, 2007), 133.

VII. Grace in Tragic Subjunctive

Black folk theology as drawn from Negro Spirituals and the testimonies of formerly enslaved women and men provides ample warrant for contemporary black theology's assertion that God enters into and intervenes in human history as Redeemer and does so, particularly, on behalf of persons who are trampled upon, who "live with their backs constantly against the wall."[189] Contemporary black theology teaches that "God discloses [the Divine Self] as Redeemer of suffering Black people in this country."[190] Yet, more than 140 years after the collapse of Black Redemption or Reconstruction, the recrudescence of white racist supremacy, the persistent irruptions of neo-lynchings or extra-judicial killings of Black children, youth, women, and men by police or their designated agents or ordinary citizens, the cunning contrivance of political policies and law continue to disrupt and dismantle Blackhuman flourishing. All the while, through willful ignorance, deliberate silence, and calculated gradualism, white Christianity sanctions this cruel concoction of the social order.

---

189 Thurman, *Jesus and the Disinherited* (1949; Boston: Beacon Press, 1996), 13.

190 Moyd, *Redemption in Black Theology*, 118. Certainly, this statement does not in any way limit divine self-disclosure; rather, it names a most crucial way in which Black people have experienced God's revelation of the Divine Self.

This matrix of calculated dissemblance, oppression, and animosity congeals as *tragic subjunctive*.

Why *tragic*? Collectively and communally, as *a-people*, African Americans have undergone "time on the cross, the lachrymose history"[191] of enslavement: "a distinctive mass experience of loss and longing, of marginalization, chronic mourning, and pain."[192] Yet African American religious experience testifies that such anguish *may* become "the site of healing, critique, and creativity;"[193] and, indeed, may give rise to a vision of the tragic, which transfigures the meaning of human existence—affirming life, facilitating "the recognition and embrace of the darker, more fundamental truths of life."[194] Matthew Johnson argues that this tragic vision assumes the "fragmented nature of our historical existence" along with a resulting aesthetic and "affective response":

> The apprehension of the tragic vision is transformative and has the effect of predisposing the subject or subject community to be receptive of

---

191 Long, "Bodies in Time and the Healing of Spaces, Religion, Temporalities, and Health," 272 of 425, Kindle.

192 Matthew V. Johnson, *The Tragic Vision of African American Religion* (New York: Palgrave Macmillan, 2010), 4.

193 Long, "Bodies in Time and the Healing of Spaces, Religion, Temporalities, and Health," 271 of 425, Kindle.

194 Johnson, *The Tragic Vision of African American Religion*, 6–7.

ambiguity, encouraging resistance to the foreclosure so characteristic of the fundamentalisms of our age. The tragic vision is a different mode of knowing. It provides a different mode of knowing. It provides a different epistemological posture. In this sense, a tragic Christianity encourages a healthier, tolerant, and more creative spiritual life, and the tragic vision is almost a necessary presupposition of an authentically democratic culture and society.[195]

Why *subjunctive*? The subjunctive denotes mood, not verbal tense or time. Usage of the subjunctive signals possibilities—anticipating, dreaming, imagining, hoping that something will (or will not) occur, may or may not come into being. Freedom, justice, equality *may* come; but Black children, youth, women, and men *live* in unfreedom, injustice, inequality. In response, Black people dream, imagine, create, hope, pray, act in and for freedom; "shift[ing] from the indicative or imperative to the subjunctive modality, endows a variety of possibilities."[196]

The matrix of calculated dissemblance, oppression, and animosity is *tragic* because white racist supremacists continue to exercise the political

---

195 Johnson, *The Tragic Vision of African American Religion*, 7.
196 Edward Demenchonok, "The Quest for Genuine Democracy: A Promise of Democracy to Come," in *Civility, Nonviolent Resistance, and the New Struggle for Social Justice*, ed. Amin Asfari (Leiden: Koninklijke Brill, 2019), 234–35.

dominance and economic leverage to limit Black personhood, impede black agency, and frustrate black hope. Yet, Black people do protest and resist and must continue to do so in overt and covert ways. Living in this matrix is *subjunctive* because such living presses Black women and men ever forward to dream, to imagine, to hope, to pray, to create, to seek truth and justice in spite of knowing that the *telos* of the American social order has been blocked against the fulfillment not only of their redemption, but the redemption of all within that flawed matrix.

Living within this tragic subjunctive cannot but challenge faith in a liberating, redeeming God.

> If God is the One who liberated Israel from Egyptian slavery, who appeared to Jesus as the healer of the sick and the helper of the poor, and who is present today as the Holy Spirit of liberation, then why are black people still living in wretched conditions without the economic and political power to determine their historical destiny? . . . Why does the Holy One of Israel permit white people to oppress helpless black people when Scripture says God came in Jesus Christ to set the captives free? . . . Is God unwilling or unable to deliver the oppressed from injustice?[197]

---

[197] Cone, *God of the Oppressed* (New York: The Seabury Press, 1975), 163.

William Jones pushes Cone's query to the extreme and asks, "Is God a white racist?"[198] Delores Williams asks and responds to the question 'How does God relate to the oppressed in history?' by highlighting the complexity and ambiguity of the biblical witness:

> The truth of the matter may well be that the Bible gives license for us to have it both ways: God liberates and God does not always liberate all the oppressed. . . . The biblical stories are told in way that influences us to believe that God makes choices. And God changes whenever God wills. But African-American Christian women are apt to declare as Hagar did, "Thou art a God of Seeing" (Genesis 16:15). And seeing means acknowledging and ministering to the survival / quality-of-life needs of African-American women and their children.[199]

Yet, even in the twenty-first century, Black people continue in vibrant faith to reach out, take hold of God's outstretched hand, and exclaim: *'We cried out to the Lord in the midst of our troubles and the Lord God heard our cries.' 'God makes a way out of no way.' 'God may not come when you call, but our God is right on time.'* How is such faith and faithful living possible

---

198 Jones, *Is God a White Racist?*, see also Anthony B. Pinn, *Why Lord? Suffering and Evil in Black Theology* (New York: Continuum Books, 1995).

199 Williams, *Sisters in the Wilderness*, 199.

in such unspeakable circumstances, in tragic subjunctive?[200] Grace. The gracious and gratuitous circumference of Divine life and love, that is, grace encircles Black being, nurtures creative possibilities, inspires imagination and creativity, sustains purposeful hope-filled action for justice in the bleakest circumstances. Blackhuman persons live and love in the interstices of *the blues* and *realized eschatological faith*.

The blues," Ralph Ellison explains, "is an impulse to keep the painful details and episodes of a brutal experience alive in one's aching consciousness, to finger its jagged grain, and to transcend it, not by the consolation of philosophy but by squeezing from it a near-tragic, near-comic lyricism."[201] The blues are neither a set of abstract ideas, nor propositional truths;

---

200 Unspeakable things happen to *all* human beings at random and by calculation. Unspeakable things have happened to Black people during slavery and continue to happen in the United States each day. Recall the murders of Philando Castile in Falcon Heights, Minnesota; of Eric Garner in Staten Island, New York; of Michael Brown in Ferguson, Missouri; of Trayvon Martin in Sanford, Florida; of Walter Scott in North Charleston, South Carolina; of Freddie Gray in Baltimore, Maryland; of Sandra Bland in Waller County, Texas; of Aiyana Stanley-Jones in Detroit, Michigan; of Breonna Taylor in Louisville, Kentucky; of Ahmaud Arbery in Glynn County, Georgia; of George Floyd in Minneapolis, Minnesota.

201 Robert G. O'Meally, ed., *Living with Music; Ralph Ellison's Jazz Writings* (New York: Modern Library, 2001), 103.

"they are the essential ingredients that define the essence of the black experience. . . . [T]he blues [are] a state mind in relation to the Truth of the black experience."[202] The blues, Giles Oakley tells us, "put into sound the feelings that are beyond words."[203]

'*I wish, I knew how it would feel to be free.*'[204] Billy Taylor's lyrics (and Nina Simone's voice) mediate the blues of Black life in struggle for life, freedom, personhood, bodily integrity, survival, flourishing, citizenship, belonging—in struggle for *ordinary* human and humane life. The blues are a way of "making bitter water, [if not sweet, at least] potable

---

202 Cone, *The Spirituals and the Blues: An Interpretation* (1972; Maryknoll, NY: Orbis Books, 1991), 102.

203 Giles Oakley, *Devil's Music: A History of the Blues* 2nd ed., updated (London Da Capo Press, 1997), 136, cited in Kelly Brown Douglas, *Black Bodies and the Black Church: A Blues Slant* (New York: Palgrave Macmillan, 2012), 7 of 187, Kindle.

204 William Edwards "Billy" Taylor (1921-2010) was a jazz pianist and performer, composer, lyricist, and educator. Perhaps, his most well-known composition, "I Wish, I Knew How It Would Feel to be Free," was co-written with Dick Dallas and became an anthem of the modern civil rights era, "Obituary: Billy Taylor: Jazz pianist who became the music's most articulate and widely heard advocate," *Guardian* [London, England], December 31, 2010, 30. *Gale Academic OneFile* (accessed November 27, 2024). https://link.gale.com/apps/doc/A245529893/AONE?u=mlin_m_bostcoll&sid=bookmark-AONE&xid=49b13d2b. The song was made famous by the musical artistry of Nina Simone.

sustenance."[205] The blues speak simultaneously of the tragic and comic in mediating a profound and profoundly complex sense of living into and with ambiguity and coherence, sorrow and joy, harshness and sweetness. To engage the blues is to endure, to accept adversity as an inescapable condition of human existence, to recognize that "there is no way not to suffer."[206] But suffering never has the last word. Hope rather than resignation or acquiescence rises in the heart of the blues.

"Heab'n, heab'n, ev'rybody talkin' 'bout heab'n ain't goin' 'dere / Heab'n, heab'n, goin' to shout all over God's heab'n."[207] The term 'eschatology' derives from the Greek *eschaton* and may be translated as 'last things' or 'end times.' The enslaved people may not have known the word 'eschatology,' but they *knew* hope and they believed that God's redemptive process would bring them into a future state in which their ordinary daily living would be free from injustice, deprivation, and discrimination.[208] So they sang of heaven and of what they would do there—sing,

---

205 Marbury, *Pillars of Cloud and Fire*, 50.

206 Albert Murray, *The Hero and the Blues* (1973; New York: Random House, 1995) 106-107; James Baldwin, "The Uses of the Blues," in *The Cross of Redemption: Uncollected Writings*, edited with an introduction by Randall Kenan (New York: Pantheon Books, 2010), 59.

207 Negro Spiritual "All God's Chillun Got a Song" is also known as "All God's Chillun Got Wings."

208 Moyd, *Redemption in Black Theology*, 232.

walk, fly, sit and eat at tables and places where they would be welcome, wear shoes and robes, and enjoy the intimate and comfortable companionship of Jesus and his Father: "*Gwine to argue wid de father and chatter wid de son.*" This Spiritual and others disclose African American eschatological consciousness which possesses

> a twofold political relevance: with regard to the difference between the eschatological destination and the present world, it drives toward altering present circumstances; and it nevertheless guards against identification of the consummation with the particular change being striven for . . . [it] becomes a power determining the present without thereby losing its futurity.[209]

This eschatological consciousness permeates everyday black life in and for the struggle for freedom: critical interrogation, challenge, improvisation, small yet concentrated acts of love and justice, daily living in such a way as to realize "the transformation of society and all creation with it from what it is to what it ought to be according to God's vision for the world."[210]

---

209 Wolfhart Pannenberg, *Basic Questions in Theology* (Philadelphia: Fortress Press, 1970), 178, cited in Moyd, *Redemption in Black Theology*, 214.

210 Karen Baker-Fletcher, "The Strength of My Life," in *Embracing the Spirit: Womanist Perspectives on Hope, Salvation, and Transformation*, ed. Emilie M. Townes (Maryknoll, NY: Orbis Books, 1997), 129.

Grace enters the tragic subjunctive on the side of black authentic living—sustaining, nurturing, lifting; neither replacing nor displacing the blues, while *breathing with* and *in* and *through* those "sad-happy songs that laugh and weep" all at once.[211] '*There is a balm in Gilead*,' sings the Spiritual, and grace pours its healing balm of love to refresh and restore *the matter* of redemption, to sustain, validate, keep hope alive in struggle.

1. Because the "gift of grace is received by a material bodily human being," grace must have bodily and material effect, must be felt in the body. "If grace does not produce material and bodily modifications, it does not exist for the human being."[212] Like a parasite, the blasphemy of enslavement with its staining inferiority and rejection burrows into and feeds on the Blackhuman psyche—consuming, despoiling, polluting. For human beings racialized as other, as slave, as begrimed and besmirched,[213] self-love, love of one's own black flesh veers close to impossibility. Yet, possibilities of new life—individual or personal,

---

211 Richard Wright, *12 Million Black Voices* (New York: Thunder's Mouth Press, 1941), 128, cited in Douglas, *Black Bodies and the Black Church: A Blues Slant*, 3 of 187, Kindle.

212 José Comblin, "Grace," in *Mysterium Liberationis: Fundamental Concepts of Liberation Theology*, ed. Ignacio Ellacuría and Jon Sobrino (Maryknoll, NY: Orbis Books, 1993), 522.

213 See Robert E. Hood, *Begrimed and Black: Christian Traditions on Blacks and Blackness* (Minneapolis: Fortress Press, 1994).

collective or communal—may be discerned and discovered in grace-sustained daring to love oneself and love others.

Grace breathes loving *redemption* of a woman's and a man's *body* to *herself and to himself*—not as an object of property or possession, but as *loved* and *loving enfleshed spirit*. Toni Morrison conveys the healing power of grace in *Beloved* through the sermon Baby Suggs preaches in the clearing. Through her call, grace breathes healing, renewing life:

> "Here, in this here place, we flesh; flesh that weeps, laughs; flesh that dances on bare feet in the grass. Love it. Love it hard. Yonder they do not love your flesh. They despise it. They don't love your eyes; they'd just as soon pick 'em out. No more do they love the skin on your back. Yonder they flay it. And, O my people they do not love your hands. Those they only use, tie, bond, chop off and leave empty. Love your hands! Love them. . . . and the beat and beating heart, love that too. More than eyes or feet. More than lungs that have yet to draw free air. More than your life-holding womb and your live-giving private parts, hear me now, love your heart. For this is the prize."[214]

Baby Suggs upends and repudiates the moralistic, dismal, soul-killing sermons directed at enslaved

---

214 Toni Morrison, *Beloved* (New York: Alfred Knopf, 1987), 88–89.

Black people, sermons that function only to reinscribe and secure the asymmetrical power relation of master and slave. Her sermon emancipates understanding, heals psychic hurt, and rends the debilitating dominance of the plantation's "fantastic hegemonic imagination."[215] The most radical imperative of Baby Suggs' sermon is this: *Love what you have been taught not to love.* This is the redemption of Blackhuman matter, the redemption of black flesh, black bodies, black lives, black living.

Even in the twenty-first century, the trauma of chattel slavery marks Black children, youth, women, and men. Psychotherapist Janice Gump explains, that this trauma entails

> the life-disruptive quality denoted by post-traumatic stress as well as the developmental trauma found within the family. The trauma may be explicit and conscious, or unavailable to awareness. It may come from society at large, as in racist acts of oppression or discrimination, or from the nuclear family. And it may be the result of trauma generationally transmitted. But infusing and determining both intrafamilial and societal traumatic acts is the historical fact of slavery.[216]

---

215 Emilie M. Townes, *Womanist Ethics and the Cultural Production of Evil* (New York: Palgrave Macmillan, 2006), 7.

216 Jane P. Gump, "Reality Matters: The Shadow of Trauma on African American Subjectivity," *Psychoanalytic Psychology* 27, no. 1 (2010): 48.

Grace prompts Blackhuman persons to identify, name, and disengage from distortions, hatreds, and alienations from oneself, one's flesh, one's body, one's Black community, and prepares them to enter into authentic relationships with self, with other human persons, with creation, with God.

2. Grace sustains hope in struggle. Hope ought to never be confused with optimism; nor is hope "an emergency virtue [hauled out] for a crisis."[217] "The black Christian tragic sense of life," writes Cornel West, "focuses on resistance and opposition in the here and now against overwhelming odds. The regulative ideal for such resistance is a kingdom beyond history, but this kingdom is ultimately brought about by divine intervention."[218] From the perspective of the tragic sense of life, African American eschatological consciousness acknowledges that suffering lies on the path to freedom and redemption; struggle recognizes its inevitability but graced black living refuses to submit to the assaults of social oppression. Blackhuman persons resist in hope. Grace supports the exercise of a person's "inner authority" in refusing "to yield the central source of

---

217 William F. Lynch, *Images of Hope: Imagination as Healer of the Hopeless* (1965; Notre Dame, IN and London: University of Notre Dame Press, 1974), 33.

218 Cornel West, "Subversive Joy and Revolutionary Patience in Black Christianity," in *The Cornel West Reader* (New York: Basic Civitas Books, 1999), 438.

one's personal consent to anyone or anything other than God," who is Redeemer and Waymaker.[219]

Grace strengthens hope in struggle—animating persons and groups as they strategize, mobilize, and act in ways large and small to stand up to the arbitrary and cruel, to denounce unmitigated power, to resist white supremacy, to withstand and stand against coercion and violence. Redemption or salvation, writes Genna Rae McNeil, "is a revolutionary spaciousness and freedom through the assertion of inner authority, breaking bonds of confinement and invalidating the reality of dead-ends." To know [redemption] "is to know through experience and faith that God will 'make a way out of no way.'"[220]

3. Hope has functioned as critical component in the psychic and existential, spiritual and religious, ethical and moral, cultural and aesthetic formation of Blackhuman persons as individuals and as a community. Hope has motivated and carried Black people through history in their discernment, imagination, configuration, conjure, enfleshment, and mediation of the meaning of being human. Black women and men lived in and out of hope, defying the bleak social

---

219 Genna Rae McNeil, "Waymaking and Dimensions of Responsibility: An African American Perspective on Salvation," in *The Courage to Hope: From Black Suffering to Human Redemption*, ed. Quinton Hosford Dixie and Cornel West (Boston: Beacon Press, 1999), 71-72.

220 McNeil, "Waymaking and Dimensions of Responsibility," 71–72.

imaginaries that thwarted their aspirations and ambitions. Hope roused and fortified them to dare new possibilities, to dream new dreams, to generate different social imaginaries, to act for future good even when its achievement proved arduous.

Womanist social ethicist Keri Day helps us to understand and appreciate hope as social practice. Indeed, she argues, "radical hope is not redemption from this world but redemption of this present world."[221] Hope synthesizes prayer and action, determination and resistance, change and transformation in and through struggle. Hope requires and affirms proper, necessary self-love, for love may materialize as a political practice. In the words of bell hooks, "To truly love we must learn to mix various ingredients—care, affection, recognition, respect, commitment, and trust, as well as honest and open communication."[222] Cornel West tells us that "justice is what love looks like in public."[223]

Martin Luther King, Jr., called such love agapic—an authentic, concrete expression of solidarity in the here-and-now yet anticipating the

---

221 Keri Day, *Religious Resistance to Neoliberalism: Womanist and Black Feminist Perspectives* (New York: Palgrave Macmillan, 2016), 166.

222 bell hooks, *All About Love: New Visions* (New York: William Morrow and Company, Inc., 2000), 36 of 272, Kindle.

223 Cornel West made this statement in a lecture at Harvard Graduate School of Education, Cambridge, Massachusetts, October 24, 2014, Facebook video.

eschatological healing, knitting together, reconciliation and redeeming of the broken and divided communion of God's human creatures. Such love grounds the initiation of beloved communities. When such communities appear as they have during the Civil Rights Movement of the 1960s in Montgomery and Birmingham, Alabama; in Koinania Farm, Americus, Georgia;[224] in Argentina during the Dirty War of 1976–1983 as the Madres de Plazo de Mayo assembled to protest the abductions of their children and family members; in Cuidad Juárez, Mexico, where mothers and women organized as *Voces sin Echo* ("Voices without Echo"), *Nuestras Hijas de Regreso a Casa* ("May Our Daughters Return Home"), *Justicia por Nuestras Hijas* ("Justice for Our Daughters"), and many other groups.[225] These communities are neither romantic nor sentimental expressions of hope and love; rather, they work to enflesh, to act, and to act out of agapic love. And such love calls for living redemption—for attentiveness and questioning, understanding and reflection, self-correction and change, judgment and decision, choice and action. Living redemption is the work of eschatological faith: it calls for curiosity, intellectual and moral commitment, integrity, compassionate

---

224 See Charles Marsh, *The Beloved Community: How Faith Shapes Social Justice, from the Civil Rights Movement to Today* (New York: Basic Books, 2006).

225 See, Pineda-Madrid, *Suffering and Salvation in Cuidad Juárez*.

solidarity, self-sacrifice, willingness to risk and to respond in responsibility. Through such love, Black human persons "offer a way of imagining futures of love, care, and justice" that neither neoliberalism nor fascism, neither oligarchy nor tyranny allow.[226]

Christian political theology alert and attentive to the registers and blue notes of the black frequency understands that redemption can never be "an abstract soteriological concept."[227] Redemption is made concrete through grace, hope, and love. Grace breathes in and through black bodies and souls, lives and minds, hearts and hands; hope invests genuine meaning in living with honor and courage in spite of being impeded or denied; love transcends and transforms blasphemous realities—always affirming living as meaningful, holy, and choiceworthy; always recognizing the presence of the Transcendent Three in each and every child, youth, woman, and man.

AFTERWORD: ENFLESHING STRUGGLE IN OUR TIME

I alter Vincent Lloyd's aphorism: Certainly, the task of the political theologian, but more importantly the task of the *free* woman and man, the *free* person, the person who desires and seeks to be *free* is

---

226 Day, *Religious Resistance to Neoliberalism*, 185–86.

227 Adiprasetya, "Johann Baptist Metz's *Memoria Passionis* and the Possibility of Forgiveness," 237.

to out-narrate domination.[228] Enfleshing struggle, living redemption as eager openness to the coming reign of God is the surest way to "out-narrate" domination. Enfleshing struggle prompts us to live as Jesus of Nazareth lived; he is *God's narration* to us, incarnating and mediating the meaning of redemption. Jesus is the standard for our exercise and achievement of freedom and redemption. He is the singular signifying example of what it means to live in solidarity with children and women and men who are poor, excluded, and despised; to take their side in struggle for life—no matter the cost. In his incarnation, he witnesses to the divine destiny seeded in *our* flesh. Jesus teaches us a new way of enfleshing what it means to be God's people, to enflesh what it means to be human, to enflesh freedom and redemption. In his fleshly self—conspicuous yet unremarkable, personal yet common, particular yet distinguishable—Jesus is made vivid through history, culture, religion, race, gender, sexuality, love, and hope. Through the power of the Spirit, he mediates the surprising and joyous end of redemption in this life and in life to come. This is redemption on the black frequency. This is what it means to enflesh redemption in our time.

---

228 Vincent W. Lloyd, *Black Dignity: The Struggle against Domination* (Yale University Press, 2022), 181 of 210, Kindle: "The task of the philosopher-rhetorician is to out-narrate domination."

The Père Marquette Lectures in Theology

1969 *The Authority for Authority*
Quentin Quesnell

1970 *Mystery and Truth*
John Macquarrie

1971 *Doctrinal Pluralism*
Bernard Lonergan, SJ

1972 *Infallibility*
George A. Lindbeck

1973 *Ambiguity in Moral Choice*
Richard A. McCormick, SJ

1974 *Church Membership as a Catholic and Ecumenical Problem*
Avery Dulles, SJ

1975 *The Contributions of Theology to Medical Ethics*
James Gustafson

1976 *Religious Values in an Age of Violence*
Rabbi Marc Tannenbaum

1977 *Truth Beyond Relativism: Karl Mannheim's Sociology of Knowledge*
Gregory Baum

1978 *A Theology of 'Uncreated Energies'*
George A. Maloney, SJ

1980 *Method in Theology: An Organon for Our Time*
Frederick E. Crowe, SJ

1981 *Catholics in the Promised Land of the Saints*
James Hennesey, SJ

1982 *Whose Experience Counts in Theological Reflection?*
Monika Hellwig

1983 *The Theology and Setting of Discipleship in the Gospel of Mark*
John R. Donahue, SJ

1984 *Should War Be Eliminated? Philosophical and Theological Investigations*
Stanley Hauerwas

1985 *From Vision to Legislation: From the Council to a Code of Laws*
Ladislas M. Orsy, SJ

1986 *Revelation and Violence: A Study in Contextualization*
Walter Brueggemann

1987 *Nova et Vetera: The Theology of Tradition in American Catholicism*
Gerald Fogarty

1988 *The Christian Understanding of Freedom and the History of Freedom in the Modern Era: The Meeting and Confrontation between Christianity and the Modern Era in a Postmodern Situation*
Walter Kasper

1989 *Moral Absolutes: Catholic Tradition, Current Trends, and the Truth*
William F. May

1990 *Is Mark's Gospel a Life of Jesus? The Question of Genre*
Adela Yarbro Collins

1991 *Faith, History and Cultures: Stability and Change in Church Teachings*
Walter H. Principe, CSB

1992 *Universe and Creed*
Stanley L. Jaki

1993 *The Resurrection of Jesus Christ: Some Contemporary Issues*
Gerald G. O'Collins, SJ

1994 *Seeking God in Contemporary Culture*
Most Reverend Rembert G. Weakland, OSB

1995 *The Book of Proverbs and Our Search for Wisdom*
Richard J. Clifford, SJ

1996 *Orthodox and Catholic Sister Churches: East Is West and West Is East*
Michael A. Fahey, SJ

1997 *'Faith Adoring the Mystery': Reading the Bible with St. Ephræm the Syrian*
Sidney H. Griffith

1998 *Is There Life after Death?*
Jürgen Moltmann

1999 *Moral Theology at the End of the Century*
Charles E. Curran

2000 *Is the Reformation over?*
Geoffrey Wainwright

2001 *In Procession before the World: Martyrdom as Public Liturgy in Early Christianity*
Robin Darling Young

2002 *Septuagintal Midrash in the Speeches of Acts*
Luke Timothy Johnson

2003 *The Reception of Vatican II Liturgical Reforms in the Life of the Church*
Pierre-Marie Gy, OP

2004 *Bioethics and the Common Good*
Lisa Sowle Cahill

2005 *"Did You Receive the Holy Spirit When You Believed?" Some Basic Questions for Pneumatology*
David Coffey

2006 *The Ecumenical Potential of the Second Vatican Council*
Otto Hermann Pesch

2007 *"Wheels within Wheels": William Blake and the Ezekiel's Merkabah in Text and Image*
Christopher Rowland

2008 *Who Are the Church?*
Joseph A. Komonchak

2009 *Theology and the Spaces of Apocalyptic*
Cyril O'Regan

2010 *Song and Memory: Biblical Women in Syriac Tradition*
Susan Ashbrook Harvey

2011 *Abraham between Torah and Gospel*
Jon D. Levenson

2012 *The Logic of Gift: Rethinking Business as a Community of Persons*
Michael Naughton

2013 *Givenness & Hermeneutics*
Jean-Luc Marion

2014 *The Christian Roots of Religious Freedom*
Robert Louis Wilken

2015 *Take Lord and Receive All My Memory: Toward an Anamnestic Mysticism*
J. Matthew Ashley

2016 *Why on Earth Did Anyone Become a Christian in the First Three Centuries?*
Larry W. Hurtado

2017 *Luther's Christological Legacy: Christocentrism and the Chalcedonian Tradition*
Johannes Zachhuber

2018 *The Perfection of Desire: Habit, Reason, and Virtue in Aquinas's Summa theologiae*
Jean Porter

2019 *History, Theology, and Narrative Rhetoric in the Fourth Gospel*
Harold W. Attridge

2021 *Understanding and Misunderstanding 'Negative Theology'*
Rowan Williams

2022 *Sensing God? Reconsidering the Patristic Doctrine of "Spiritual Sensation" for Contemporary Theology and Ethics*
Sarah Coakley

2023 *Philosophical Reflections on Śabad (Word): Event—Resonance—Revelation*
Arvind-Pal S. Mandair

2024 *Christological Hellenism: A Melancholy Proposal*
Lewis Ayres

2025 *The Politics of Redemption: The Doctrine, the Matter, the Law, and Grace*
M. Shawn Copeland

About The Père Marquette Lecture Series

The Annual Père Marquette Lecture Series began at Marquette University in the Spring of 1969. Ideal for classroom use, library additions, or private collections, the Père Marquette Lecture Series has received international acceptance by scholars, universities, and libraries. Hardbound in blue cloth with gold stamped covers; some reprints with soft covers. Regular reprinting keeps all volumes available.

Ordering information:
Marquette University Press
Toll-Free (800) 247-6553 fax: (419) 281-6883
Online: www.marquette.edu/mupress/

Editorial Address:
Marquette University Press
PO Box 3141
Milwaukee WI 53201-3141
phone: (414) 288-1564
web: www.marquette.edu/mupress/